# Anthology 2025

## Bayside Writers' Group

Copyright © 2025
Bayside Writers' Group
All Rights Reserved

ISBN 978-1-7637654-1-2 Anthology 2025

ISBN 978-1-7637654-2-9 Anthology 2025 (eBook)

This publication may not be reproduced, stored in a retrieval system, or transmitted in whole or in part, in any form or by any means, electronic, mechanical, photocopying, recording, or otherwise without the consent of the author(s). Inquiries should be addressed to the publisher.

Published in Australia
Printed by Ingram Spark

**Anthology 2025**

*Authors*: Aileen Heal, Amanda Divers, Ann Simic, Anne Sedgley, Caroline McCrindle, Dianne Motton, Dita Gould, John Aarons, John Breden, Judith E Dowling, Lorraine Doney, Lucy Tomov, Maeve McGoohan, Monika Nuesch, Paul Downton, Peter Levy, Rose Lumbaca Crane, Roslyn Evans, Sharon Hurst, Su Lam, Zhiling Gao

Design: Sharon Hurst
Cover photograph by hello aesthe at pexels.com

# Acknowledgements

I would like to extend my heartfelt thanks to everyone who contributed their work to this anthology. Your creativity and commitment have made this collection possible.

This has been a wonderfully successful year for the group, with new members joining and vibrant discussions enriching each of our meetings. We were also privileged to share readings at a number of aged care and retirement facilities, where our words were warmly received and deeply appreciated.

Our sincere gratitude goes to The Brighton Library for their generosity in hosting our meetings and for their ongoing support of our group.

If you would like to become part of the Bayside Writers' Group, connect with any of the writers featured here, or contribute to future editions, please contact us at: baysidewritersgroup@bigpond.com

# Contents

**Aileen Heal**
    The power of words ................................................. 1
    Mythical ................................................................ 27
    Golden childhood ................................................. 60
    Why poetry .......................................................... 88
    A fragile friendship ............................................. 123
    Sacred Unravelling ............................................. 147

**Amanda Divers**
    Prarabdha ............................................................... 2
    Theaceae .............................................................. 25
    The White Sentinel ............................................. 41
    Peace ................................................................... 59
    Sophia ............................................................... 113

**Ann Simic**
    Perchance poetry ................................................ 20
    Love (after e.e. cummings) ................................. 21
    On rising ............................................................. 71
    This tower .......................................................... 94
    The die is not cast ............................................. 116

**Anne Sedgley**
    Judith .................................................................. 53

**Caroline McCrindle**
    Five minutes of fame .......................................... 90

**Di Motton**
    Local transport – Indian style ............................. 97

**Dita Gould**
    Shumlek's story .................................................. 24

**John Aarons**
    Belated birthday greetings .................................. 74

**John Breden**
　　Garic, the lost hound of the darkness ............... 42
**Judith Dowling**
　　The man in the greatcoat ............................. 3
**Lorraine Doney**
　　Off to the war ...................................... 28
　　I for Isabel ........................................ 80
　　A Christmas Tale ................................... 120
**Lucy Tomov**
　　Beach ............................................... 26
　　Sweetness ........................................... 51
　　Teenage manspreading ................................ 58
　　How to exist ........................................ 72
　　A love letter ...................................... 101
**Maeve McGoohan**
　　Thriving – a first day at school .................... 62
**Monika Nuetsch**
　　Talamira the beautiful princess ..................... 22
　　Senior love ......................................... 82
　　Time travel ........................................ 114
　　My nightmare as an au pair ......................... 130
**Paul Downton**
　　all this spinning! .................................. 19
　　I hear .............................................. 32
　　Bring me my ear trumpet ............................. 73
　　Look at me .......................................... 96
　　Morning on the bay ................................. 127
**Peter Levy**
　　The most troubling challenge for
　　modern humanity: Disconnection
　　in an age of hyperconnectivity ..................... 124

**Rose Lumbaca Crane**
  Being a witness ....................................................... 23
  Comparing............................................................. 52
  People ................................................................. 79
  Can a café be a friend? ....................................... 102
  I'm in love........................................................... 128

**Roslyn Evans**
  Easter 2025 .......................................................... 31

**Sharon Hurst**
  Skeletons........................................................... 103

**Su Lam**
  The Forest Ghoulie.............................................. 118

**Zhiling Gao**
  Coming to Australia .............................................. 33

## The power of words

There is nothing more powerful than words.
Words can transport you to another time and place, another dimension.
Words from the right leader can win battles.
Words can soothe an aching heart.
Words can turn an ordinary day to extraordinary.
Words can weaken the strong to their knees.
Words between two people can forge two hearts.
There is nothing more powerful !
Except maybe…..
One touch.
Then perhaps there is no need for words.

***Aileen Heal***

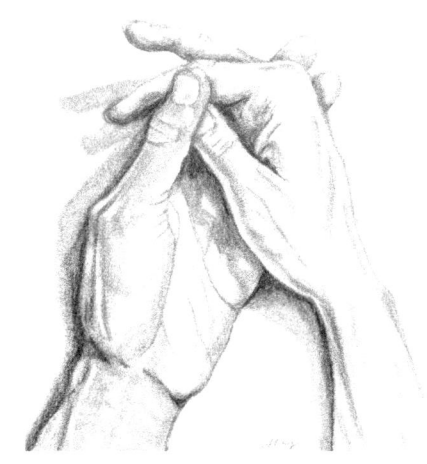

## Prarabdha

You speak in spite, just for the thrill,
Deception's high—you chase it still.

But fear has made you raise your chin,
For if you glance at where you've been,
You'll see the scorched earth in your wake—
The cost of every move you make.

But time, it turns with silent grace,
And reckoning will know your face.
While I walk clear with quiet pride,
You wouldn't know this truth I bide:

The weight you sow will one day bloom,
Its petals sharp, a fragrant doom.
For justice waits in patient hue,
And shadows come to claim their due

**Amanda Divers**

# The man in the greatcoat

'You're hurting me Mumma!' Josie was yelling. Her mother, Miranda, clutched Josie's shoulder and with it a clump of her hair, tightly, forcing her head back. Miranda was in her own frenetic world as she sided one shoulder, then the other, forward into the crowd. Her breathless calling was whispered pleading.

'John. John!'

Over and over again.

A brutal train blocked the daylight as it pulled into the station, leaving only a grey mizzle for a foreground. Men in khaki coats, with kitbags on their shoulders, poured onto the platform. Miranda now clutched Josie's wrist and jerked her this way and suddenly that. The little girl kept her head low to protect herself and tried to get her hands to her face. Her red beret was pushed from her head and was trampled under feet. She pulled at her mother's arm but was yanked forward. Nobody heard her cries. She wore new clothes, so many of them that her arms wouldn't bend. Her new shoes were a size too big and her heels were sore from rubbing. She kept her fingers clenched to stop her gloves falling off. The empty knitted fingers jutted out like little deformities. Miranda made gasping sounds. Her grip changed and again she held onto Josie's clothes at the back of her neck.

'Choking Mumma. Choking!'

Miranda was tall, now she seemed taller. She loomed over Josie. She seemed to be all legs and arms and stretching, swaying body. Josie's body felt like nothing but a soft pudgy cushion being poked and pummelled to fit the shapes she was being wedged into. Miranda kept calling this name. John, a stranger's name to Josie, yet one she had often heard. It belonged to someone over there, out of sight. She had never before heard this high-pitched John sound. Now it was an urgent 'John', sometimes soft, sometimes long and loud and it came out amid excited little squeals. Miranda's face was blotchy pink and white, her chin jutted forward and her neck was craning.

Something was wrong. Josie felt the jolt of an unexpected stop followed by stomping and scuffling of feet. When Miranda let go of her hand, her head was pushed into rough fabric. Metal buttons dragged at her face and hair, like fingernails in need of cutting. A man was crushing her mother and trying to crush her too. He swung Josie into the air once, twice, three times. His strong hand pressed her face to his chest. She screamed and arched her back away from him, his smell and prickly coat. She stretched her legs down and wriggled to the ground, then lunged away from him, hauling her mother's jacket with her.

'I'm here Mumma. I'm here. I've got you. Push Mumma. Push!'

She turned and forced herself between them, pushing them apart, this huge man-shape and her mother. She sucked back saliva and kicked his legs again and again, until he stood back from Miranda and held Josie at arm's length, out of reach of her kicks. Her mother bent and heaved her up to rest heavily on her hip. Josie wrapped her legs tightly around her mother's waist, wriggling to get under her jacket. As she did so, Josie felt herself squashed up against the man. He tried to keep his face next to hers and give her kisses, unbearable prickly, sweaty kisses. She punched out at his forehead and dug her fingers at his eyes. Her last weapon was her teeth. She clamped her teeth into his cheek and stretched the skin out from side to side. Wild-eyed and shaking, she bit into him with all the force she could muster. Blood trickled down his face, mingling with homecoming tears.

They said he was her father.

'Get up Josie darling. Get up and let your father see you.'

'Away. Just go away. Take him away.'

Josie lay on the tram seat, full length, on her stomach and hiding her grubby face. The man who was her father put his hand lightly on her back.

'I've come home Josie.'

'Don't touch me. Don't look at me.'

She got up from the seat and slapped away his outstretched hands. In red-faced fury she yelled at him as she claimed both of her mother's hands in her own.

'And don't you touch her either.'

'Give her time John. It's all so new.'

"It's not. It's not. I don't want that man.'

He called her his Little One, his Sweetheart, his Angel.

"I'm not Angel. That's a stupid name. I'm Josianne and I belong to Gran and Mummy. We don't want you.'

Miranda did want him, and he wanted her. They walked slowly home from the tram stop. Miranda and the man wrapped together and Josie lagging sulkily behind.

'He's not staying at my house,' she called.

She ran up from behind them kicking again at his legs and trying to separate their arms from each other. She wanted to be carried – by her mother. Grandmother appeared on the street, hurrying, waving and smiling. Josie ran to her, but she made 'wait a minute' signs. Grandmother walked past, then huddled together with Miranda and the strange person Josie was quickly realising was going to have to matter in her life.

They stopped at the gate, walked up the path and through the front door. The man carried his bag straight to the bedroom, the big room at the front of the house that Josie shared with her mother. He put the bag on the bed. He stayed. He knew where the kitchen was. He knew without being told where to find the soap in the kitchen sink cupboard and exactly where the teaspoons were kept. He knew about the birds in the aviary outside. He even said the camellia had grown. He wanted Josie to show him this and that, her toys, the new wireless, where she would like to have a vegetable patch. 'Show me', he said, holding out huge brown hands.

'When's he going?' she asked.

Grandmother took Josie away to the kitchen-bedroom where Aunty Jeanie Webster slept whenever she came home. A heavy dark red curtain had been hung, dividing the room in two. Grandmother showed her a narrow bed and a chest of drawers full of her clothes, in the part of the room that was to be, as Grandmother said, all her very own. On the bed was a new blue eiderdown and under a new pillowcase was her nightdress.

'Those don't belong there,' said Josie.

Grandmother distracted Josie with whispers she had to strain to hear. The two sat on the bed. Josie buried her face in her grandmother's softness.

'You and I have been invited next door. For tea. We'll leave your Mumma and Daddy here to get to know each… Marion's making Mella. Mmmm. Nice Joey?' said Grandmother.

'And chocolate ice cream?'

'Let's go and see. Coming?'

Grandmother held out her hands towards Josie. Those hands were somehow always warm. Josie knew them well. She knew the creases that formed as Grandmother massaged them with hand cream, to keep them soft and make the little brown blotches go away. She knew the bluish veins of each hand separately. Sometimes, like on this day - particularly on this day - those hands were very strong.

They stayed a long afternoon and evening with the neighbours, Marion and her parents, who Josie knew as the Birdies. It was much longer than they had stayed visiting before. Marion's dad never smiled and although Josie didn't look at him, she could see out of the corner of her eye that he had hair growing out his ears. They pulled chairs closer to the Radiola and listened to 3AW. They laughed at Daddy and Paddy then sighed listening to 'When a Girl Marries'. Grandmother closed her eyes and hummed the song that was always played at the beginning and end of the program.

'We'll have a nice cocoa before you go, and Marion can show you all the little ornaments in her shadow box. You'll love that. Little china cats and dogs and things. Just lovely,' said Marion's mother.

Marion's father looked at his watch. Josie shuddered because he let out a huge chortle, the sort of laughter that showed no sign of happiness. Miranda had said several times that Bob Bird was an uncouth person and now Josie understood what she meant. Grandmother had said the same thing too once, about some men travelling on the open-air section of a tram.

'No hurry,' he guffawed, patting his wife on the bottom. 'You two won't be missed. Oh no you will certainly not be missed. Oh, ho ho no.'

'I said this didn't belong here,' said Josie grabbing the nightdress on her new narrow bed. 'And that's not my bed. Not. Not. Not.'

It had been a long day, the day the man arrived, but despite her tiredness she was revived by the mention of bed. She trailed the nightdress through the house and stuffed it under one of the pillows on the big bed in the big bedroom. Two more bags of belongings had arrived for the man. They were open, and their contents were spilling out. Clothes, both his and her mother's, were strewn about the bedroom. Miranda's new jacket was almost hidden on the floor under the bed. Her hat was sitting on top of the vase of roses she had picked early that morning, before the train station, before the man, before the misery. Josie found an earring on one pillow and a necklace under another, and her mother's new skin-coloured petticoat ruffled up with the sheets. Strangely enough, one of her mother's precious silk stockings was hanging down from the ceiling, caught up in the light fitting. The man's big coat was hanging over the wardrobe door nearly covering all the mirror and other clothes were in a pile in the corner. There was a new perfume fragrance, a wet towel and talcum powder all over her mother's dressing-table. Josie stuffed anything she didn't recognise into the bags. She dragged them out of the room, taking time between her efforts to kick them and call them flaming nuisances. It was late, eleven o'clock and Josie was beginning to lose her little war against sleeping in the little bed. The last she remembered of that day was sitting on Jeanie's bed hearing Jeanie's story-book voice droning on and on about a princess and a pea.

As much as she wished it, the man didn't go away. She knew the uneven rhythm of his step – a clip then a clop – and the odd stiff-legged way he walked up and down steps. She occasionally quickly glanced at the red and brown places on his legs between his socks and his trousers where she had kicked him. How she could have made such marks with her kicking was beyond her. She had tried kicking a slim tree trunk near the front door. Her mother had said that she had to be gentle with things in the garden because they were living things and like people, would be spoiled if they were hurt. Perhaps tree trunks were different because she had kicked the tree trunk several times but only once made a slight mark. Nothing like the dints and scars on the man's legs.

New cooking smells wafted about. She'd watch the man from the corner of her eye as he shovelled huge fork-loads of food into his mouth, never leaving more than the odd bone to be thrown out. Before he ate, he would always thank God for the food. Before letting her raise her fork to eat he would try to settle Josie by holding her hands down in her lap. Josie tensed her whole body and pulled her hands away. He would sing 'Thank you for the world so sweet. Thank you for the food we eat' – that one – looking at her with wide eyes. Come on Josie, join in, he'd say but Josie never did. She always looked the other way, at the wall or out the window. Josie only sang it softly at night in bed. Soon her father stopped singing that song and muttered other words before eating. He muttered and

Josie just let the words roam loose in her head.

He stayed, all night. Every night he stayed in the big bed with her mother. Josie peeped. They were there although she couldn't always see her mother's dark curly hair. They made a lump in the bed, a big untidy mess of a lump so she couldn't tell what was him and what was her. She saw skin. They told each other stories and played games. Sometimes, it seemed he was rough, hurting her and making her cry out and when Josie could bear it no longer, she would go in and push the man away. She would yell at him angrily, tell him to lie still, stop the silly games. Come to my bed Mumma, I won't hurt you, she'd say. She watched at the doorway and bit into her lips. I am soft and small, my skin is smooth, she wanted to say. My hands won't drag your mother parts and make you squeeze your eyes in pain. Remember me, Mumma.

Why they sometimes laughed at her was unfathomable. Grandmother only tut-tutted when Josie begged her to send the man away because he was sometimes cruel to Miranda in the big bed. The aunts just giggled. It was Jeanie who told her that men and women – married men and women – always slept in the same bed. Girls always slept in their own beds and kept their nightdresses on all the time. When a girl got married she could show a man her legs and her boosies and let him play games with her. It was called sex. She said there were two sexes and what happens is this you see, the man and the woman really like each other, and they want to be really, really close. Then their skins touch all over, you see, and they start to do a sort of dance, lying down, which is very exciting and they dance until they get really exhausted. That's what.

Josie walked away – it was all a bit silly. All she cared about was the fact that the man was still there.

'I don't care', she said, 'about why they do all that sexes business, I just want that man to go away and do it somewhere else.'

In the evening, she was tucked into her little bed very tightly and she had to fight herself free. She could hear muffled voices in the kitchen, sharpened by the noise of a stream of water, the whistle of the kettle, dishes being washed and stacked. She strained to follow every sound and every conversation – the high tones of the young woman, her grandmother's lower softer voice and the man's richer rounder tones. Every word he spoke she resented. She listened and followed their movements as they sat around the kitchen table. Pouring the tea, replacing the sugar bowl lid, stirring, putting the spoon back in the saucer, sipping, putting the cup back, and sighing with the pleasure of it all. The only sound she disliked was that of the man crunching gingernuts. It sounded like steps on gravel. She counted biscuits.

Before he retired for the night the man would stand by her bed watching her. She squeezed her eyes shut and when he touched her face or hair she squirmed away under her eiderdown. When she woke in the night she whispered loudly to Jeanie. If there was no answer she's get up and feel Jeanie's bed to see if she was in it. If Jeanie wasn't there, she'd feel a flash of panic and run to the big bed. Sometimes she would drag her eiderdown with her and curl up in it on the floor by her mother's side of the bed or she would stand by her mother twiddling her curls, never sure if she wanted her to wake or not. The man often wanted to carry her back to bed but he never managed to. Only Miranda was permitted.

'Stay Mumma. Tell me a story.'

Miranda stayed a while and told a story.

'No more Joey. Your Daddy's waiting.'

Still the man didn't go.

'Hop in Little One', he said when he found her standing by the bed at night.

He sat up and stretched over to lift her up. She refused and thumped her fists on his legs. He grimaced and left her alone.

'Not his legs Josie. You mustn't hurt his legs. Never again. Do you hear?'

When she was allowed in the bed she curled up at her mother's side, and into her mother's shape and stretched her arm around her waist pulling her away from the man. Sometimes when she was touching her mother, the man's skin would also be touching her mother's and would touch hers too. She would bring her arms into her chest or turn over and try to feel of her mother's radiance. In the mornings she would find herself back in her own bed and wonder how she got there.

The man wore a uniform, and his shape filled the doorway. Each day he went out, but always came back. Josie always felt annoyed to see Miranda powder her face and comb her hair at the mirror and watch out the window for him. One day another man in a uniform knocked at the door and her father went away with him in a car. He didn't come home, not the next day or the next. Miranda said he had gone away to the army hospital.

The house had been full of him, his books, his newspapers, his chairs with untidy cushions, his clothes on the doorknobs, the tools he used to fix things about the house. Josie could no longer smell him in the big pink bedroom.

He no longer burst in the door and made her mother laugh. He wasn't there to ask Josie for kisses and not there for her to refuse him. She wondered if he had gone away because she had wished him away. She began to watch for him from the front window then she ventured to the gate, then further.

Twice she climbed into his wardrobe. She pulled the door closed and sat in the dark sniffing his clothes, especially his big coat. She would stroke it and run her fingers around the buttons. It was a horrible smell, she told herself, but she filled her lungs with it, relishing a slow and dreamy in and out, in and out. She had always loved her mother's smell. Hers was of powder and perfume but his was marvellous, foreign and mysterious. Hers sat lightly in the air and wafted from place to place. His was more like a protection that stayed and wrapped itself around you.

Miranda asked Josie to come to visit the man at the hospital. She shook her head. No.

'Don't worry about it Miranda', Grandmother said. 'Give her time. Here Josie. Come to Gran. Come be my girl.'

The next time she was asked she said no but meant yes. Eventually when she saw her mother in her hat and coat, she appeared with her own and shrugged her shoulders when they asked if she wanted to come.

A large sign said Repatriation Hospital. Everything was painted green, even the crisp sheets were green. The man smelled of soap and his face was shiny clean. His eyes were blue and wettish, as he watched her. Josie asked her mother what was wrong with him. 'Go on', Miranda said, nodding to her, 'Ask him yourself. Ask him Joey.' Josie looked at the floor - she had never spoken to him before. When she looked up her mother was gone. She'd left the room, and

Josie was alone with the man. He just watched her and patted the sheet for her to come closer. She turned her back to the wall and felt his fingers touch her back. She moved from his reach to the bedside chair and sat with her hands wedged under her thighs, swinging her legs and practicing her whistling. Josie noticed his bandaged legs and thought about the dreadful day when she first saw him. She remembered how she kicked him, bit him. She thought about his clip-clop walking. She squeezed her eyes to imagine the hurt.

'Is it sore?', she wanted to ask.

Instead, she pursed her lips, whistled in a breath and frowned.

'I'll give your mother a kiss and she can hand it on to you. Ok?', he said.

Josie shook her head.

They left the hospital. Josie skipped along in front of her mother then turned to take her hand and hurry her along.

'That's the end of him', she thought.

∼∼∼

Josie was wrong. She didn't connect the birth of a baby brother with the man at all. Not all the lumps in the bed or the dancing with touching skins. The little boy was Nathaniel, but she called him Nat. He was made for her, and she loved him. She kissed him endlessly because she wanted him to feel that she loved him more than anyone else did. She had wanted a black baby but Miranda had said she couldn't promise that.

'What's your new brother like?' asked the not so angelic-looking Marion from next-door.

'He's mine Marion and you can't have him. You can't even see him.'

'I suppose he's pretty ugly, eh?

'He's a Chinese baby but it doesn't matter', she replied.

'Chinese!'

'Chinese babies are best, Marion.'

'Honestly Josie', said Marion shaking her head and tutting. 'You're only five. You don't know anything. Do you?'

'Do so! Anyway, go get your own baby Marion.'

❧❧❧

She had been to see the baby at the hospital. A sign said Children Under Fourteen Not Admitted but a nurse appeared at a window, pulled open a pink curtain to hold up the baby for her to see. Josie pressed her nose to the glass. That's the first thing she noticed about Nat. Chinese. Grandmother said he had a lot of dark hair for a new-born and that he was ever so slightly jaundiced.

'Jaundiced is good. Isn't it? Very good, Gran?' said Josie.

It was a long walk to the hospital where her little brother was born. Grandmother talked with the man all the way. Josie ran a stick along the fences but stopped when the man took hold of her hand. Josie pulled away. She ran ahead then came back and walked next to him poising her hand for him to take again. He didn't and she wished he would. She really wished he would.

She shared Nat with the household. This, she decided to allow, because she was not tall enough to do everything for him herself. When she went to claim the crying baby from his crib the man told her not to touch him or when she lifted him up, the man came to claim him for himself. The others in the house did the same but that didn't worry her as much. She watched Nat every chance she had. For hours she looked at him. She didn't notice changes in him or that he no longer looked Chinese.

Josie had plans to steal the growing baby and take him far away. To a place even secret to her. She seemed to be endlessly waiting to get taller. Nat seemed to be heavier every time she carried him. She nurtured her mind's picture of a larger Josie and a smaller Nat. When she looked at herself in the cheval mirror wearing her mother's hat, and when she tilted the mirror so that her image filled the glass, she saw Nat's real mother. She took her claim and carried him as far as the tram stop. Beyond that she had no further plans and by the time the tram stopped, and the conductor said, 'Well girlie, on or off?', Nat was crying, and he had pooed his nappy, so Josie said 'Off'.

Later when both Josie and her brother were bigger, she would drag him from his cot and take him into her bed. She covered him up to his chin with her eiderdown and twisted his dark hair around her fingers. He would turn to her and let his arms and legs rest on her skin. As he slept, she listened for his breathing. His little chest rose and fell noticeably but sometimes his breathing was so light she had to stop her own breathing to follow his. As he lay still and silent, her heartbeat thumped at her throat as she imagined him dead. She nudged him to make him stir. She was always compelled to check.

Josie had to check a lot of things, she even had to repeatedly check that she had ten fingers. Time was bringing her to the realisation that the dragons and gargoyles on the roof most probably did not move any more. Nevertheless, she liked to check that they were all there, in exactly the same positions. Hadn't those ugly monsters come into the house? Hadn't they often fought over who was to eat her and who was to take the first bite?

Josie loved to pretend she was someone else, not merely a small girl encased in the security of her family in a substantial red brick house in a city suburb. Miranda and her sisters had a wonderful dress-up trunk from their childhood, full of ragged bits and pieces of costumes, hats, hand-me-downs, laces, curtains and half-finished dressmaking experiments. When she draped any conglomeration of these articles on herself, she believed without a second thought that she had become someone else. At five years old she wore these things with the promise of a natural flair. She could quite expertly curl her hair into bobby-pins and wore hats at rakish angles. She liked to be a pirate, an Indian princess, an explorer or a world-famous gymnast who was adored by everyone. She thought she looked especially marvellous as a girl soldier who had been so brave she had been given a medal.

Added to her dress-up collection was an old army shirt and a light brown army cap with a leather band. This was her captain's hat. It had that old tobacco smell of the man. It was one of her favourites. When Nat had taken the shape of a little boy and was no longer just the joining up of fat round tubes she started to contrive costumes for him. The women of the house always thought he looked beautiful, but the man told Miranda not to allow Josie to torment the boy.

Little Nat also took a liking to the brown cap. Josie put it on his head and held him up to the mirror. She gave him dozens of kisses and pressed his face to hers. She picked up her hairbrush from her chest of drawers and put it in his hand telling him to hold onto it tightly. Nat waved the brush around because, as Josie told him, he was a brave soldier fighting the enemy. Josie held his arm and guided it to her face.

'Scratch me Nat. Go on, scratch. Hit. Make it hurt.'

The boy jabbed at her with the wire bristles of the brush. He arched his back away from her hold and jabbed harder.

Josie winced but said, 'Harder Nat. Scratch harder. I'll forgive you.'

She pressured the brush into her skin and dragged it down her face. Blood surfaced in dotted lines. She put her hands to her face, smeared the red and tasted it.

'I love you. You're my sweetheart, my angel. I forgive you,' she said, and she covered his face with kisses.

**Judith E. Dowling**

## all this spinning!

spiralling
through the heavens
slung out on an arm
of this pinwheel galaxy
hurtling through the space-time
of now

keeping our distance
from a solar oven
cooking up matter
from nothing
moving
impossibly fast

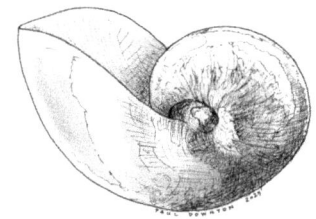

holding fast
to a rock with a heart of fire
rotating within its thin skin
of nebulous
constantly moving
atmosphere

all this spinning!
all this!

that we might turn together
lips to lips
on this still and gentle evening
to seal our love
with a golden kiss
in the dizzying sunset

**Paul Downton**

## Perchance poetry

Speeding down the murderous Moorooduc to Mornington
on Saturday at 10am, the coveted prize of poetry awaits —
perchance? No chance — a deserted desert of bitumen,
no car at all but mine; a lone man on a bench in the sun.

With shrivelling heart I disembark,
greet the boy on the bench with
"Not again".

I sit with him in April sun warming to
emptiness. I met him last time when
poetry ripened in a nearby room.

We commiserate; I realise a message
must have circulated since no one else
arrives. But I had carefully checked
to avert another misspent morning.

Here is a new trial, a deficit to dampen
my ageing being but — I find his name
is Niall, about the age of my sons;

I hear a small slice of his uneasy life —
I see that this was meant to be, that he
is now the poetry, that this bench may
hold sweet souls who entrust another.

He lives just down the road, an easy
walk — we talk, he talks, until it's

time to drive him to the place he
wants to go on his lone path —

and continue my journey to the
pragmatic poetry of the weekly shop.

**Ann Simic**

## love    (after e.e. cummings)

longer than life
stronger than trees
roughly remembered
shorter than sharks
fair as fortitude

reckless    mysterious
alive beyond everest
beyond sceptics

less than a race
more than life
less than grace
more than rage

love lingers
bumps and sways
continues infinite
**simple as simon**

**Ann Simic**

# Talamira the beautiful priestess

In a quiet village nestled between two large mountains, lived a beautiful young priestess.

She was graceful, her touch healed, her voice soothed and every man who caught a glimpse of her fell under her magic spell.

The women though in the village became frustrated and jealous; and one of the elders had a plan.

We need to banish her from our village. They all eagerly agreed to this plan.

Solstice day is coming up, a perfect opportunity to arrange a female gathering.

We will entice her with a lovely cup of magic mushroom tea and a piece of cake. That will send her into a deep trance and then we can transport her to the dark pristine lake in the ancient forest.

In a bag we will give her some food and clothing. And when she wakes up, she will read a note that says:

"Never come back to our village."

The Priestess Talamira remained by the lake.

Some say, on moonlight nights, her soft voice rises above the lake and some even say they saw her spirit figure rising from the lake.

Many men travelled this path from far away just to get a sighting of her beauty and hear her enchanting voice.

*Monika Nuesch*

## Being a witness

Observe in silence, do not stir the pot, listen to your instincts, trust
Witnessing people's behaviour from a distance
Learning to watch people from a distance
Without judgments, observe and learn
A glimpse of what makes them say and do
I hear what they say
Get a hint of what they don't say
They utter nice things
They utter not so nice things
Reading their body language
Reading their patterns of behavior
Could they have an agenda
Being vigilant and observe
Protection and learning, wait for the answer
From reliable sources and a sense of knowing
Be silent and watch people from a distance
My instincts were mostly right
I was reluctant at times, not wanting to trust the wise little voice within
So I paid a price, something I needed to learn
Some people are nice and some are not so nice, some are both within moments
Things to consider while being vigilant and observing people from a distance

**Rose Lumbaca Crane**

# Shumlek's story

My funniest friend was always busy; we skied together and sang all the way down the ski slope. Apart from manufacturing he brought entertainers from overseas to Australia (Melbourne) and I helped him to sell tickets.

Unfortunately, he had a very difficult life during the Holocaust. He and his younger brother were the only two in his family to survive Auschwitz. Wherever in the world he travelled, he would ring people in the phone book with his name, to see if they were related. In London there were two people with his name.

He rang the first one and started to explain. They must have thought he wanted something from them, and promptly hung up. It took him a day to get up the courage to ring the second one. On the phone they realised they were not related, but the Londoner invited him for dinner, where he told them about the previous encounter.

His hosts were most upset and plotted a revenge. They told Shumlek to call the first people and tell them that he brought a large sum of money for the heirs of a namesake. He told them he had found them, and then promptly hung up.

*Dita Gould*

## Theaceae

She stands in silence, dressed in fire,
A whisper born of earth's desire.
Each curve a secret, soft and sweet,
Each shadow bending at her feet.

The winter yields beneath her gaze,
Yet still she blooms in muted days.

Her petals—lips?—will not confess,
Yet all the world leans close to guess.
And though the frost may seek her grace,
It melts when meeting her embrace.
For beauty born of fragile flame
Defies the cold that speaks her name.

Yet time will sip her crimson hue,
And scatter pearls of fallen dew.
What lingers then—a dream, a trace,
A ghost of light in empty space.

**Amanda Divers**

## Beach

I write love letters to
strangers on trains
as though I am a matriarch
holding her children
close as something horrific
passes through quickly. I whisper,
look at your hair! How swiftly it shuffles
over your shoulders! I couldn't wear
earrings like yours but how
beautiful they are, I hope you feel
the warmth of a hearth over your back because
it will dispel the fickleness
of your tired knuckles and others' attitudes to your
auburn hair. We can have a good day
under our sun, laid out over
the shining grains of
glass sand. Glass sand, my,
isn't that odd? A shard sharpened and whittled down
for years until it sticks and falls
into the break between your finger and its bed.
Even after so many years, it
inconveniences you so!
Come here, I can kiss it better!
Stay close and I'll watch
you paint my freckles,
with your eyelashes,
with the watercolour pallet you bought.
How well you draw, sweet love,
now cover your ears and
let
**it all**
**pass**

**Lucy Tomov**

# Mythical

If I could –
I'd make you wings
Painstakingly sew each feather
Even as my fingers bled
So you could wear them
Watch you rise like a Phoenix
Emblazoned. Empowered.
Out of the darkness
To shine your light bright.
But you are not a mythical bird.
You are you.
Quirky and insecure.
Hard on yourself.
Creative and kind.
Humble in your beauty.
Perfect in your imperfections.
If you could only see
The light I see –
For you are more than a Phoenix.
Wonderful you.

***Aileen Heal***

# Off to the war

On the third of September, 1939, Bob, his wife, Olive and their two children, Lauren and Tom gathered around the wireless to hear the voice of the Prime Minister, Bob Menzies.

'Fellow Australians, it is my melancholy duty to inform you officially, that in consequence of persistence by Germany in her invasion of Poland, Great Britain has declared war on Germany.'

'I told you it wouldn't be long before Hitler made another move,' Bob said. 'Next thing we know, Menzies will be sending our troops overseas.'

The children sat quietly. They didn't like to hear talk of war. At the subsequent call-up, the unemployed flocked in droves to enlist, including Keith, the children's uncle. Melbourne streets pounded with the footsteps of soldiers, eyes looking ahead to a grim future. Marching, marching like they'd never marched before. Crowds lined the streets to farewell the soldiers, some with tears in their eyes, at the thought of their sons and husbands leaving them, while others were proud, their heads held high.

On the day Keith marched off to war, his wife, Bertha stood in Bourke Street, with their sons, Johnny and Donny. She waited until she saw Keith march past, then with sons at her side and tears in her eyes, they caught the tram home to Richmond.

As was his custom, Bob had his ear tuned to the wireless.

The news wasn't good. The Japanese had occupied Rabaul, New Britain, Papua, New Guinea.

'Isn't that where Keith is?' Olive asked. She had a terrible feeling that Keith was in trouble.

'Sh!' Bob said, 'I'm trying to listen.'

The voice of the Prime Minister, John Curtin, filled the room. Japanese fighter planes had flown over Darwin and rained bombs on the city. The enemy was close. Bob was alarmed. What if the Japs moved southwards?

Behind the scenes, the Prime Minister had picked up the phone and demanded to speak to Mr. Churchill, the Prime Minister of England. No. He would not release the Australian troops. They were needed to defend England. Another phone call, this time to Mr. Roosevelt, the President of America. Yes, he would help his Australian friend. John Curtin, breathed a sigh of relief.

Something was wrong, Lauren and Tom came home for lunch to find their father on the back porch, a piece of paper in his hand. After he read it, he removed his glasses and wiped his eyes, while their mother sought her husband's shoulder to lean on. She was in tears. It was a telegram from Bertha. Keith had been killed in New Guinea.

A flock of cockatoos flew overhead piercing the air with their screeches.

Bob looked up. All he saw was Keith, his body covered in blood dying in the arms of a comrade. Keith, his mate. Keith the life of the party. Bob wandered down the backyard, the telegram still in his hand. He read it again, endeavouring to digest the news it contained.

Alarmed by the news, Lauren watched the water dripping down the sides of the Coolgardie safe. The last time she had seen her uncle, his foot was bloodied and he was grinning at the sight of it. And now he was gone. Why hadn't the prayers she'd said for him in Sunday school saved him. Where was the God she'd been told to pray to?

'How will Bertha manage without Keith?' Olive said. 'She's always leant on him.'

Tom hung his head. 'Poor Johnny and Donny,' he said.

> Private Keith Stenhouse, aged 29, Unit 2/12 Infantry Battalion, killed at Sanananda, Papua New Guinea. Husband of Bertha, and father to John and Don.

**Lorraine Doney**

## Easter 2025

Leaves in my street are turning once again.
Crepe Myrtle hints at fiery red; apple tree competes with gold and brown.
What account can I give of the gift of these last twelve months?
Hours of fear and pain in nights at Holmesglen hospital
Have given way to a rich embracing of a life of gratitude.
I wash and dry my light grey hair, pleased at the image that stares back from mirror.
I take deep breath and strike D on timpani for the Mozart Overture, while full orchestra adds its simple harmony.
I hear delight in shouts of my neighbours' boys at their basketball ring
Blending with wattlebirds' call and screech of white cockatoos
As they herald the end of day.
My 11-year-old twin grandsons stand tall as I mark their annual growth on wall chart.
My 16-year-old granddaughter and I swap ideas on Duolingo for Japanese and French.
Opening car windows, I accelerate to Abbots St beach.
Resolutely, I stride to water's edge, keep walking up to my knees, plunge in.
My legs and arms go numb as I stretch out and swim in ecstasy towards horizon.

***Roslyn Evans***

## I hear

I hear terror on live-export ships
I hear jet skis on the surf
I hear a thousand chainsaws
levelling the Earth

I hear the hum of data hubs
pretending to be clouds
engines of destruction
veiled in sexy shrouds

I hear the hiss of bitumen
spread thick with seething cars
I hear loud talk of leaving Earth
and paving over Mars

I hear exploding ordnance
tear holes in nature's skin
I hear the voice of living things
cut short when they begin

I hear loud voices rant and rage
with words that should be ours
I hear their meaning loud and clear
in the sound of dying stars

**Paul Downton**

## Coming to Australia

In 1987, as I rattled toward my future aboard an old steam train through the vast landscapes of Inner Mongolia on my way to Beijing Airport, my stomach was full of dumplings, and my mind was full of possibilities. Nervousness flickered briefly, a quiet echo of the unknowns awaiting me in Australia, but mostly, excitement surged. This was the beginning of a new adventure.

Once aboard the plane, the air hostess led me to a seat beside a tall, elderly Australian woman. I sighed with relief, the mix of anticipation and excitement bubbling up. It wasn't just about my first Western meal; it was everything that lay ahead. As the plane roared to life and accelerated down the runway, it suddenly hit me, this was real, and the adventure was finally underway.

Before leaving home, I had searched high and low for information on how Westerners use knives and forks, but the only thing I could find was a small column in the corner of the local newspaper. It said that Americans use the knife in the right hand to cut their food, then switch the fork to the right hand to eat. English people, on the other hand, hold the knife in the right hand and the fork in the left to cut and eat without switching. But what about Australians? The article didn't say.

When the small box of food in an aluminium container arrived, the sweet old lady picked up her knife with her right hand. I picked up mine with my right hand. She took her fork in her left hand. I did the same. She cut her food. I tried to cut mine, but my knife wouldn't go through. Then I stared at her moving the knife back and forth like a saw. I copied her motion. Success. We brought the food to our mouths at the same time.

I closed my eyes and savoured the tender, juicy meat. It was heavenly. *This* was what I'd been missing in life. Right then, I decided I was going to *love* Australia, because I already loved the steak. It was like my taste buds had just discovered the meaning of life. I had a terrific feeling about the new life ahead: kind and friendly people, delicious food, and even a modern movie playing on the large screen in front of us: *Crocodile Dundee*, and there were Paul Hogan and Linda Kozlowski kissing, right there on screen, without anyone worrying it might corrupt the youths.

ৡৡৡ

I settled into a quiet, leafy suburb called Kew East. The next morning, while exploring a nearby street, I came across a church. I had seen one before, years ago in my grandma's village, but that church had been converted into a stable during the Cultural Revolution and used to house horses.

Curious, I approached the door and peered inside, cautiously. Growing up, Communist propaganda had portrayed churches as dark, sinister places, dens of long-bearded Western spies disguised as priests and nuns, lurking to steal state secrets or test drugs on innocent children. But now, I wanted to see what real priests and nuns looked like.

I stepped carefully through the entrance. It was empty. Slowly, I walked further in, stopping halfway down the aisle. The silence was deep. A crucified Jesus hung at the front above a hollow podium. A chill crept up my shoulders. Suddenly unnerved, I turned and ran out the door.

Outside, a ray of sunshine warmed the chill from my shoulders. I reassured myself that there was nothing sinister about churches here. It was just the lingering weight of the propaganda I'd grown up with, but my god, it had been powerful.

A woman stood at the side of the road. She had a large belly and wore a bold, fluorescent green and orange coat. In her hand, she held a long stick with a pink circle on top.

Having just come from a country of over a billion underfed, skinny people, I found myself drawn to plump figures. I watched her with quiet admiration, her fair, supple skin, full stomach, and strong legs. She looked like a lucky person, someone who had plenty to eat.

My grandmother would have thought her the most beautiful girl in the world, if only she'd had long plaits. *"Beautiful girl, big and fat with long plaits,"* Grandma used to say.

I stopped and watched her, burning with curiosity about the purpose of this plump, fluorescent-coated woman holding a big stick by the side of the road. A moment later, another woman emerged from the gate of a building next to the church, it looked like a school. She smiled at the lady in the fluorescent jacket, and the lady smiled back.

I quickened my step and caught up with the woman.

'What does that lady do?' I whispered.

'She is the lollipop lady,' the woman told me with a smile.

My English wasn't fantastic, but I knew the word *lollipop*. What a wonderful country, I thought. They even hire a lollipop lady to hand out a lollipop to each student before school starts.

A month later, I moved into a shared house with Lian, another student from China. We became good friends very quickly.

Lian and I were thrilled when an Australian woman she knew invited us to dinner at her house one Saturday evening.

'It will be so much fun to see what Australian families are like,' said Lian, 'but this Australian lady said something really strange.'

'What do you mean?'

'She asked us to bring a plate.'

'*Aiya*, that is strange,' I exclaimed. 'Why can't she just borrow plates from her neighbours like my mother did when we invited people over for dinner?'

We didn't have plates, only bowls, so we went to Target and bought two small plates. We didn't want to seem too greedy by bringing large ones. Lian put on her pretty sky-blue dress, and I wore my favourite white dress. We stood in front of the mirror together, combing our hair and getting ready for our big night out.

'Here, put this nice blue clip in your hair,' she said, while placing a large green one just above her forehead to hold back her annoying fringe.

I did the same. 'Where did you buy this?' I asked, admiring her green clip while securing the blue one in my own fringe. In our culture, wearing matching clothes and accessories really cemented a friendship.

A friend of ours offered to drive us to the dinner. Lian and I walked to the nearest junction and stood near the curb, waiting. The gentle Melbourne breeze lifted the hems of our dresses, swirling them softly in one direction. With our bright, colourful hairdresser's clips in place and a plate each tucked carefully in our handbags, we looked at each other and smiled. We felt beautiful and glorious.

Then I looked up and saw a red sign above us. As was my habit, I read it carefully, anything to improve my English.

*No Standing Anytime.*

I pointed it out to Lian and told her what it said.

We both quickly sat down on the curb.

Finally, our friend pulled up in his car and stopped beside us.

'Why were you sitting on the curb?' our friend asked.

'Because the sign told us to,' I replied, feeling proud to be following the rules just like any true Australian.

But he laughed and explained that the sign only applied to cars, not pedestrians. We all burst out laughing.

We arrived the same time as many other guests came in carrying large plates of food, which they added to the table. With horror, Lian and I suddenly realized what "bring a plate" really meant. Well, I'd learned English, or so I thought, but obviously, there was more to it. We didn't mention the small plates tucked inside our handbags and tried to be as inconspicuous as possible, all while sporting our large, colourful hairdresser's clips.

The party was truly a feast – an impressive long table piled high with plates of chicken, beef, lamb, pork, and a variety of fresh salads, a level of decadence that many Australians might not even realize.

One Australian lady asked us where we got our large hair clips. I told her that Lian had bought them from the hairdresser. She made a little face, and Lian and I glanced at each other.

*Was there something wrong with our hair clips?* we asked each other with our eyes. We both leaned in to examine each other's clip. Then we grinned and shook our heads. No, nothing wrong with our bright blue and green, oversized hairdresser's clips, we decided. They looked great.

The momentary fashion doubt couldn't dampen our happiness, not with mountains of delectable food laid out on the table. There's an old Chinese saying: *If you have plenty of food and tea, nothing can possibly be wrong in the whole wide world.* And in that moment, that's exactly how we felt.

Just as we were patting our stomachs and feeling full, the hostess brought out plates filled with creamy cakes. Lian and I looked at each other in amazement. *There's more food?* The cakes looked absolutely delicious, but I had eaten so much meat and salad, I didn't have any room left.

ಲಿಲಿಲಿ

A few days later, I bumped into my neighbour Lisa and her adorable, bold-headed baby, Angelique. Her husband Bill was off at work, probably working hard to pay for all the baby clothes with "mysterious stains" on them. I stood there for a while, playing peekaboo with Angelique, who was surprisingly good at it, considering her lack of hair.

Lisa then invited me in for a cup of tea. We sat down and started chatting about her baby.

Suddenly, Lisa turned to me and asked, 'What are you having for tea?'

'For tea?' I blinked, confused. 'Like… the drink?'

'No, silly,' she said. 'What's for tea?'

I scratched my head. 'Uh, maybe some biscuits? I'm not

sure… What *do* you have for tea?'

'I'm cooking roast lamb!' she replied proudly.

'Oh, so you mean dinner?'

Lisa looked at me like I had just suggested she was speaking Klingon. 'Yes,' she said slowly, 'dinner'.

I smiled awkwardly, well, I'm making rice and pork stir-fry for dinner. You Aussies really love confusing everyone by calling dinner "tea," huh? But I didn't say it out loudly.

༒༒༒

One Saturday afternoon, Lisa popped over for a visit. We were chatting away when, after a bit, she excused herself to use the bathroom. A few minutes later, she emerged with a perplexed look on her face.

'Your toilet smells… really nice,' she said, clearly impressed.

'Oh, yes,' I replied casually, 'I put a few drops of perfume in there.'

Lisa blinked at me like I'd just suggested I sprinkle fairy dust in the bowl. 'Why would you put perfume in the toilet?'

I shrugged and explained, 'Well, when I bought this pair of really fancy stockings from Myer, the shop assistant gave me a complimentary bottle of toilet perfume.'

Lisa stared at me, unblinking, as I went to fetch it from my bedroom. I proudly presented the bottle to her. 'See here,' I said, pointing at the label. 'It says: Eau de toilette.'

Lisa exploded into laughter like I'd just told her I wash my socks with champagne. 'You're kidding me,' she gasped between giggles.

'I swear, my mother used to do this all the time back home,' I said, still defending my "refined" toilet habits. 'She'd put a few drops of perfume on the floor of the toilet.'

But as Lisa was laughing her head off, I couldn't help but wonder if my mother's theory about Western people was just as wrong. You see, she once told me that she'd heard Westerners kept . . . rubber wives.

***Zhiling Gao***

## The white sentinel

Beneath the moon, a phantom stands,
No chain to bind, no mortal hands.
His coat, a shroud of winter's breath,
His eyes, twin flames that challenge death.
No trumpet sounds, no banners wave,
Yet kingdoms sleep in dreams he gave.
For on the hill, through storm and night,
He keeps the dark from tasting light.

The world may turn, the years may fade,
But still he haunts the twilight glade.
A loyal oath in silent stone—
To guard the gates that aren't his own.
They whisper tales where shadows creep,
Of one who wakes when others sleep.
A spirit forged of frost and flame,
No man can tame, no time can claim.

***Amanda Divers***

# Garic, the lost hound of the darkness

My name is Garic, and I am one of the Gwyllgi, the dogs of darkness. I was once a proud member of the Cŵn Hyfaidd Newydd, the Hounds of the Wild Hunt. In those days my master was Clud ap Gwyn the Lord of Hyfaidd Newydd and the Master of the Wild Hunt.

### *The Wild Hunt*

Well I remember those happy days of yore when twenty or so of we majestic black hounds would silently pad off in our pack. With us, mounted on their coal black steeds, were the Wild Hunt Hunters, the knights and earls of Hyfaidd Newydd. I recall with relish the euphoric, excitement I felt, as we passed from Tir Marwoleth to the Earthly Realm and prepared to begin the hunt. I breathed in the fresh earthly air and soon felt the joy of catching the scent of our quarry, and hearing the blare of the horns of the hunters. Then we Cŵn raced forward towards the scent, and the horses prepared to follow.

How magnificent we of the Wild Hunt looked, as we raced before the icy wind, with our large red eyes like pools of blood, our scarlet ears laid back against our heads and our long black fur swirling about us in the wind. Every time my mouth watered, as the tantalizing odor of my prey titillated my senses. I remember well cornering each and every prey, horrid misshapen creatures that they were, but so delicious to the taste as I sank my fangs deep into their raw bloody flesh. Oh happy days.

Unhappily, one day, when the Wild Hunt was in full cry, I was drawn by a strange scent away from my pack. I wandered for a while till suddenly I realized I could no longer hear or smell my pack and I knew not where they were. I was lost and I knew it. I sat down on my haunches and howled into the night, as I had been trained to do, and I waited for the Whippers-in to come for me. But none came to find me.

My life had changed forever and not in a goodly way. From then I had to feed myself and make do with tracking and killing poor tasting earthly animals. At first I stayed in the forest, where I was left behind, scrounging for this poor tasteless food. However, one day I noticed some robbers had set up a camp in the forest, and curious as I was, I crept close to their fire. They were horrible, murderous, ruffians, the scum of the earth, which I could easily tell from their smell. I knew that if any one of them was to die they would become my true prey, but I could not bring myself to kill one of them as, in that form, they looked so much like my masters.

But finally I was in luck. For one day, two of the robbers had a falling out and one killed the other. Even as his spirit rose up from his body I began to smell the creeping necromantic ooze coming to his spirit and sticking to it giving it physical flesh and form.

The smell was maddening, so like the smell of my prey. But I controlled myself and waited until he had mutated into one of the Sluagh. (The Sluagh are creatures formed from necromantic residue combining with the evil dead spirits of humans.) They are our prey and taste like ambrosia, the food of the gods, to us the dogs of darkness. The moment he was fully mutated I leapt on this sluagh and devoured him. Strangely he did not die. I did not know until then that such creatures cannot die, for they are already dead, their flesh is but the product of evil spirit and magic. I found I could feed off this thing for a very long time, and I did, for the more I ate the more his flesh grew back.

After some time, the robbers began to sometimes behold me in the forest, and they grew very afraid of me, which was good. Soon after this, a number of solitary human travelers began passing through these dark and lonely woodlands. Sometimes, if I felt like it, I would pad along behind them. I would not leave them until they exited the forest. The travelers may or may never have known that bandits had been watching them and would have murdered and robbed them if not for their beholding my presence. I began to do this quite a bit, and later I learned that tales of guardian black dogs had become quite common around the forest where I dwelt.

One fateful night I heard the sound of hounds in full cry and the blare of hunting horns. I crept close to determine if it was the Wild Hunt and my pack. So close did I come that I could behold them in the distance. It looked a bit like the Wild Hunt, but the huntsman was not my master Lord Clud, the hunters all wore red fur coats and the dogs were not my pack. These dogs were smaller and shining white, although they did have our scarlet eyes and ears. I crept away and they never noticed me. However, the following day, when I went back to where I had feasted on one of the Sluagh, I found that it was gone. They must have been the wild hunt after all, but oh, how things had changed.

### Lonely Roads

After that I left the forest and went where humans dwelt, not crowded too close together, especially lonely farm houses and small towns and villages. At first I was attracted to grave yards and funeral parlors, though I soon learned that my prey would not stay there long. As soon as they mutated into Sluagh they were gone. I discovered instead that hospitals and prisons were better places to wait for evil people to die. Sometimes if an evil person was mortally wounded I could just wait around battlefields for them to die. I also learned the smell of evil people who were just about to die, and I would just wait around their doors until they passed.

One night I saw a young woman walking along the road with a giant mastiff by her side. Suddenly a riderless horse bolted past her and almost knocked her down. Being the curious beast that I am, I sidled closer to her until eventually she noticed my large blood red eyes studding her in the dark. She called to her mastiff and tried to set him upon me. But the terrified mastiff just crouched and whined piteously at her feet.

However, I, feeling no fear, walked right up to her. She did not smell of death but there was something strange about her smell. Then suddenly her foot came out at me as she kicked me as hard as she could. That was a bad idea. The kick did not hurt me; indeed there was little that could. But instantly a circle of silver fire rose up about me and I sat back on my haunches and howled at the moon. She had activated the spell that could send me home and I could almost smell the air of Tir Marweleth. All that she needed to do was speak the words Hyfaidd Newydd and I would be home, but alas she knew not those words.

The right leg of the woman, which she had used to kick me, was suddenly burnt black and paralyzed, and she had fainted away. I quietly got up and slowly padded forth.

**The Chase**

In the towns, occasionally, I began to meet others of my kind but they were very wary and unfriendly until one night as I shall now explain. It was late one evening when I beheld a farmer exit the tavern in Marchwiel. Gusts of icy wind blew through the town ruffling my fur. Still I felt not the cold, for creatures such as we generate our own heat inside and never feel the freezing touch of winter. The farmer at first seemed unsure as to whether he should proceed or go back to the roaring fire within the tavern.

In the end he went forward and struck out towards the gate that led into the fields. It probably was a shortcut he had used many times to reach his home. In any case, as was my want, I followed along behind him at a goodly distance. The farmer did not catch site of me, for it is difficult to behold one such as me in the dark, for my coat is as black as coal and I was stealthily silent. Not only was it dark, but it had been raining hard all day and a fine mist was still held in the air.

However, when the farmer reached the gate, he seemed to change his mind. Instead of entering into the fields, he set off along the road, with me padding along behind. He probably thought the lower fields would be flooded from the rain, and did not want to wade through mucky fields. He walked quickly and I could hear that he was humming a little tune, no doubt to distract himself and keep up his wavering spirits.

After some time I made an involuntary noise and the farmer stopped and tensed and peered intensely in my direction. For a very long time he stood very still glaring right at me, but I too stood still and he beheld me not. He cried out something, I knew not what, and prepared to defend himself from harm. But luckily at that moment a cow appeared not far from me. The farmer laughed at his fear, for he assumed it was the cow that had coughed, as cows are want to do. The farmer turned and walked on and I silently followed too.

I am not sure why I was following the farmer, as he did not seem to be evil and there was no smell of evil or immanent death upon him. If humans are evil and they are going to die soon, that is a very good reason to follow them. I can smell the evil of their lives as well as I can smell the smell of death. I can follow and watch and wait as the necromantic magic begins to collect on their bodies even before they die. Once they are dead it grows and mutates on their dead spirit which shall provide a tasty meal for me.

There are, however, other good reasons to follow humans. Sometimes when I follow humans they have been known to kindly provide me with food. Still perhaps the main reason to follow humans is because I am a hunter who loves the thrill of the chase. Perhaps this farmer's fear would overtake him and cause him to run and then I could give chase. In any case, I continued to follow the farmer, curious to see what would befall.

As I followed, I beheld small animals scurrying out of the path of the farmer. Then a fox slunk out of a hedge and crossed the road the farmer was on and vanished into a field. After some time, the farmer turned off the road along Cock Bank into a small lane, which presumably led to his house. The lane led downhill and was densely flanked by bushes and trees and the farmer began to make good progress.

But after we had proceeded thus for some time, the farmer suddenly stopped. He seemed to notice something moving behind him. He turned and peered furtively back to the rear. Then all at once a howl shattered the quiet of the night, and I knew at once that it was another of my kind. It was another of the Gwyllgi, for a large black dog shaped shadow crept out of the trees and into the center of the lane behind the farmer.

We are, I must say, very impressive and fearsome looking hounds and this creature was even more impressive. He was much larger than most normal dogs, with large flashing white fangs. His flame like ears were laid back against his head, and his large eyes shone bright red like burning coals. He was truly one of the dogs of darkness. Indeed I recognized him, as the hulking brute revealed himself to the farmer. This was Black Shuck a hound known to be mighty, even among us, who are his kind.

The farmer began to run. He passed a clay pit filled with water and then the clouds cleared for a moment and there, caught in the moonlight, was yet another huge Gwyllgi. It turned to look at the running farmer and at that moment I leaned back and howled into the night. Almost as if by magic more of us black dogs poured out of the trees. I recognized many of them. There was Gurt, Gytrash, Grim and Padfoot. With one mind we all started to run, and the chase was on.

All of us raced behind the farmer in full cry. Our paws pounded along the lane and our breaths rasped with our efforts as we struggled to catch the farmer with every fiber of our being.

### The Iron Bolt
But the farmer strained every sinew in his body to run like the very wind. Yet still we were gaining on him coming closer and closer. He was a mere few feet away. We were almost upon him when he reached his farmyard. Then he got a second wind; he charged across the yard and through the kitchen door. Quickly he bolted that door with iron and stopped us in our tracks. We could follow no further for iron barred the way.

### The Pack
However, I felt wonderful. It had been so long since I had felt such joy. No, it was more; it was something I needed to do. Maybe the others felt the same. We were bred for this, we were trained for this, we needed to do this.

I looked about me; the chase had brought us together. I wondered if perhaps we could stay together. Yes, as I looked around they did not seem to be eager to slink away. They were, like me, sizing each other up. Some were sniffing each other.

What was that? One of the pretty bitches was looking at me. The moment I noticed her, she turned away pretending to be uninterested. And what was that? She flashed her hind quarters at me. That was interesting to say the least. I had not thought of females or sex in a long time. I had prided myself on being alone. But this group was good. I did not know what I was missing until now. I needed the chase; I needed the pack. We were pack animals after all.

We did not need to chase frightened humans, we could chase the Sluagh. It was us who sniffed them out, it was us who ran them down. As a pack we could hunt the Sluagh by ourselves. What need had we of the master? What need had we of the huntsman and the hunters? We could chase down the Sluagh and gorge ourselves on their ambrosial flesh.

We should stay together and hunt the Sluagh. Perhaps I could convince the others of this. We could be the hunters and know again the thrill of the chase and the joy of the hunt. We must stay together. We shall stay together.

I looked around; we looked around at each other with a feeling of satisfaction in our hearts. I knew in that moment my life had changed forever. We, the dogs of darkness, had become a pack again.

*John Breden*

## Sweetness

As I get older
I feel my own
misguided sentimentality caught in
the apricots which
years ago
hung from our neighbour's tree,
like art for the penniless.

We always began the operation
in the soft worn palms of my father's hands
as he turned the fruit over in the metal mixing bowl.
Cold water was best to wash with,
a serrated knife was best to cut with, and
the smaller half was best to eat first.

He pretended not to look when
my tiny sisters snatched up whole fruits and
cackled. Their blonde curls catching sunset,
their faces stuffed with sweetness and glee.
Once the mess was made, he'd bring out
paper towel to dab at our lips and say gently,
*you grubby little girls!*
All the while
we'd be playing cymbals with the pits.

The orchestra we conducted,
the ritual so delicious,
the stains unimportant.

He belonged to us; we belonged to him.
Oh, apricots.
Oh, springtime.
Oh, our dad slicing fruit
in the twilight dim.

**Lucy Tomov**

## Comparing

We might be taller
We might be
shorter We might
be lighter We might
be heavier She
might have this He
might do that
What makes us different, what is it that makes us similar
One thing for sure we all suffer in different ways and in degrees
So why hurt the other and self
How to stop the hurting of others and self
If ok with ourselves we don't need to hurt the other
When we all have our crosses to bear, how to lighten your load?
Learning from the masters of life throughout history makes sense The masters of good thought, right words and living
This lightens my load, making my life easier
So I have chosen to learn from the masters throughout history
The ones that are smarter and wiser than I and others
Then I think about how I can cultivate more happiness

**Rose Lumbaca Crane**

# Judith

Judith was always a worry to us. I say "us" as if there were a group of us over here, and Judith across the room, back to the wall, facing us. This is indeed the way it was, but perhaps only in my head and Judith's.

When I started work here, she was tirelessly kind, explaining procedures, purposes, people till my head whirred. She is on more teams and committees than I could number; she initiates more groups than there are staff in the library, and is "pushed around by them" all. All this while protesting her innocence, her exhaustion and her longing for peace.

"Hello, Anne. How are you?" she will cry, hand to her forehead cupping a headache delicately: with the other, a full 18th-century sweep towards a chair (straight-backed, grey vinyl).

I resist the urge to sway down onto it, adjusting my crinoline.

"Not bad. How's things, Judith?" I lean over the back of the chair experimentally. It tips.

"We are surviving." Then, gathering pace, "Today has not been good. Thirteen Washington airfreight bags arrived today – and Janice is on leave, Irving away with hay fever and Karyn has classes all afternoon. I shall have to lug the bags around myself. I hope Mr Charlesworth calls in this afternoon to see to what desperate measures we are reduced."

(No matter how strongly she felt, Judith's grammar was always correct).

It was nearly eight years since the first time I heard this high grandeur, this tone of brave despair, undershot with accusation:

"We will do our duty as officers and gentlewomen, but if the world knew the quality of the balaclavas they have supplied us with, there would indeed be questions asked."

That first time I was deeply shocked,

"But *surely* if they *knew* you were in here on Sunday trying to clear the backlog, they would give you more staff? Can't *I* do something to help?"

"No no!" A hand sweeps up arrestingly. "No. It is *most* kind of you to offer but you have your own pressures and priorities. No. It is management's responsibility and they have abrogated it."

That silenced me. Abrogated.

"They know. They know. I have told them. I saw Mr Dawe coming into the building on Sunday as I was leaving and I said to him gaily, "Just arriving, Mr. Dawe? Some of us have been here since morning service, tending the coalface."

Her room on the fifth floor has two glass walls, one facing east across to the distant hills, the other south over the elms and poplars of the Fitzroy Gardens, past the towers, floodlights and skyscrapers of the city, across to the bay itself. On wild afternoons, the southern sky fills up with glittering grey cumulus, and storm light slants across the cathedral spire. The trees are green and gold, the clouds are dazzling white and dark slate against a threatening deep blue sky. Gulls drift over the treetops while the sparrows outside our window ledge chatter in anxious little groups.

In spring the pittosporum hang out their scented white bells till the Gardens reel with their sweet heavy fragrance. You can smell it through the glass 200 yards away. In spring you'd swear every second tree was a pittosporum. They alternate with *Grevillea robusta* (the Silky Oak), and the glory of the Gardens, the avenues of elms.

The elms begin by pushing out along the length of their cracked black branches little scrunches of torn, pale-green paper. When the seeds are ready to float away, the leaves come: brilliant emerald-green against the black, the youngest, freshest, frilliest leaves shimmering out of the oldest blackest branches. Then come the glowing candles of the horse-chestnut flowers and the tall golden profusion of the *Grevillea robusta* flowers. The coal-face isn't too bad.

But Judith is up there, toiling along a narrow tunnel, dragging the truck uphill on hands and knees, where even a yellow canary would turn spectre-thin and die. She is checking incoming mail, sorting out labyrinthine matters of detail. The Hot Springs Agricultural Experiment Station at Broken Valley, North-West Arkansas, sends us two copies of their journal on exchange and another on subscription. We have received only one copy incorrectly – it should have gone direct to Applied Geomechanics – but which of the exchange copies is this unnumbered issue in hand, and to whom should we write about the two missing copies?

Judith has inexhaustible energy, unquenchable fatigue. Meticulously accurate about detail, she sends typed memos, paragraphs-long, to other Section Heads, outlining the problem-as-she-sees-it with consummate skill, specifying precisely what the other person needs to find out, and stirring up a demarcation dispute with every memo. This she denies.

"I know they think I write too much. But these are the questions we need answered. Elvie's not one, as you know, to put herself out: she hasn't reviewed the Hot Springs A.E.S. exchange balance *ever*, as far as I know. They cancelled three titles in 1983 and 1984, and we are still sending them our most expensive and prestigious titles, unquestioningly. It's not my job to tell Elvie how to do hers, but I simply want it to go on record that there *are* these problems of supply, compounding the problem of inequitable exchange. Still, who am I to wonder why? We must just soldier on . . . My head is terrible today, simply terrible."

"Have you tried earplugs?"

"Geoff ordered me some but I threw them away after the first five minutes. They increased the ringing in my eardrums and irritated the middle ear. And they were green."

"Pity," I nodded. "Blue? Would blue have been better?" Then quickly, "Sorry, Judith. I'm not making fun of you. Or only very slightly. I'm sure it's awful. But couldn't you just put down the dates of receipt, the issues not received, and leave it to Elvie to spell out where to go from there? It would make things easier for you."

"I know, I know." She collapses in her chair, curved over by the weight of being Judith in an ungrateful world. Suddenly, she sits up.

"I've got something for you. It's a coloured brochure about a new, authoritative edition of the Duc de Berry's *Book of Hours:* two volumes, definitive, superb full-size colour plates, scholarly analysis of different theories regarding the three scribes whose hands can be detected in the manuscript, and a full exegesis on the iconography of each page, with detailed comparisons drawn with contemporary illuminated manuscripts in the British Museum and the Louvre. $895.50 the two volumes. A cased set."

Judith knows everybody's interests, everybody's details, everybody's history. "Of course you know her mother was married before? To one of the Baillieu-Myers? That explains her love of music and the arts."

Judith is an astonishingly energetic switching-point, distributing material to several hundred people, to each according to his or her line of country, or spouse's line of country, or children's current passion. Where does she learn all this? She is the grapevine so it's not from that.

But she is not a gossip. She cares about other people, and is interested in every detail about them. She fans many spot-fires into life, taking it on herself to defend others, despite their protests. You could not help liking her and being irritated, in equal measure.

Late in my time there she developed Meniere's Disease, which severely impairs balance and creates nausea. Judith attributed this directly to stress in the workplace, which management should have detected and prevented. She died *of* it or *with* it, I'm not sure which. But I miss her patrician attitudes, her warm affection, and her energetic commitment to life and its injustices.

**Anne Sedgley**

## teenage manspreading

sit stiff
upright patriarch in your
blue-green suit and tie;
tied up behind the lectern.
you don't look like it; knees spread
on the train.
but you smell like it;
Lynx Africa and
old cans quarter-full
in the bathroom cabinet.
tortured young;
combed and left there.
abandoned
in front of the promised land.

*Lucy Tomov*

## Peace

In quiet hours when the heart feels still,
I trace the cracks that time did fill.

The words once sharp, the silence wide,
Now softened by the turning tide.

I send a whisper on the wind—
"Forgive me, friend, for where I've sinned."
No louder voice, no grand display,
Just hope that peace will find its way.

To every soul I've hurt or lost,
I count the lesson, not the cost.

And in the light of healing grace,
I make my peace, and give it space.

For bonds once broken, if made true,
Can bloom again—reborn.

***Amanda Divers***

### *Golden childhood*

Take me back to a golden childhood
Where the days dragged their feet,
but lived in the moment.
The future seemed so distant
and dreams did not just whisper,
but dared to breath life.

No heavy mornings placing a mask
to face a day filled with responsibilities.
Just days seeking sunshine
and the next adventure.
Spirit too wild to sit in a comfort zone,
with curiosity a constant companion.

No tiptoeing around egos and expectations
in case speaking your own truth
fractures invisible fragile bonds.
Connections were not complicated
and nothing ever felt forced.
The soul too thirsty to ask for permission.

No hormones to swing moods,
hidden feelings or emotional struggles.
Only a friendly hello in the playground
enjoying the company and imagination
while playing, with no expectations.
Carrying a force that could not be subdued.

No past regrets that linger like the chill
of autumn holding you back.
Childhood trust and wonder worn
like a shield that always believes

something wonderful will happen.
Knowing even small things were magical.

Those days were golden for a reason.
The air was filled with promise
and even the sun shone brighter.
Keep trying to reconnect
with that inner child because
Adulting can be very hard.

**Aileen Heal**

# Thriving – a first day at school

The launch of 1965's little greenhorns into the Big Wide World was not the least traumatic for their parents. Far from wailing at the blue door to the schoolyard, the Irish Catholic Mammies, for it was always the Mammies, skipped down the steps with winged feet, delighted that the Catholic nuns had finally taken yet another toddler off their hands. Most had several even smaller greenhorns at home.

The nuns, for their part, were on a mission to do God's holy work, and it's fair to say they did indeed make work of it, very hard work. But they were well equipped. The nuns gave big-eyed glares through bottle-end glasses. They had hard hands and thick leather belts with long key chains clinking against black rosary beads which hung from the middle of their black shrouds. One had fingertips covered in sticky tape due the wounds wrought by calligraphy and another, when animated, spewed little bubbles of spittle out of the corners of her mouth. They all terrified the living daylights out of me. Surely it was nuns such as these who inspired J.K. Rowling's dementors.

Now that's not to say the nuns didn't have their hands full. Most of the new girls were tame, if untrained, but a few, especially the country girls, were positively feral. Concepta Boyle was one such kid. The nuns were used to low level, 'shuffling behind the mammy' resistance, and indeed bitter tiny tears, but not so much the savage, winner takes all approach displayed by this wee newbie.

In a sort of pre-emptive strike, Concepta or Cepta literally kicked the whole day off with a heroic swift jab of her new brown Clarks into Mother Ignatius' thick, varicose-veined right ankle. It seemed Cepta had some misgivings about being dragged away from the warmth of her Mammy, who had not left the building. Cepta had no intention of being guided to sit on the floor of the drill hall with the rest of the navy-clad novices. She was going home with Mammy. There were others among us who would have liked to go home with their Mammies, but none rebelled with the ferocity of Cepta Boyle.

Although violence featured heavily in her own slim portfolio of teaching strategies, Mother Ignatius wasn't at all used to other people initiating combat, and for a moment it looked as if the little mite might get the better of her. Unaccustomed though she was to such ferocity in four-year-olds, Mother Ignatius rallied well, and the attack triggered a reflex response to slug away at the back of little Cepta's legs with her huge right hand.

"Behave, you little brat!"

This appeared to have worked, in fact initially it did, and the audience of Cepta's tiny peers held our collective breath, certain that the nun had prevailed. Not a bit of it. What the rest of us saucer-eyed onlookers mistook for acquiescence was merely Cepta pausing to draw breath, putting the key in the ignition, before smashing full throttle into fifth gear. With a glass shattering scream "Fuck Off" she lunged at the nun, dragging the massive black tablecloth of a veil to reveal a smooth, white head.

Now I'd often heard my Mam saying, 'Everybody knows their own' and Mammy Boyle knew Cepta's scream a mile away. Having heard the call of the wild, the curvy matriarch was compelled to turn and bound back up the steps she'd just descended, towards the shrieks of her beleaguered offspring. St Philomena's was Bridie Boyle's own Alma Mater, and she'd been the recipient of many a wallop from Iggy. Hardly surprising then, that Ma B had fighting form in this particular amphitheatre and relished the opportunity to play lioness to these particular Christians. But even Ma Boyle must have been shocked at the tableau before her.

The puce-headed nun and the toddler were engaged in something of a running battle between the open drill hall door and the carbolic smelling toilets further up the brown linoed corridor. In an uneven, sideways tug of war, the enormous black veil serving as a rope, a David and Goliath type skirmish ensued, thrilling all us littlies, and giving us pause to consider our own refugee status. Maybe we should not have come quietly after all? But still this was craic you wouldn't like to miss. Context and timing account for a lot in life and in 1965 no one in our townland even had a telephone, much less a television. Entertainment of this calibre was hard to come by. You had to hand it to the nuns, they certainly got bums on seats, or in this case, on the floor. In truth the fracas could easily have been settled if the holy woman had merely relinquished her firm grip on the shredded veil in one hand, and Cepta's little arm in the other. Except that was never going to happen. Relinquishing anything, from her virginity right through to a reluctant pupil was simply not in Iggy's character, or indeed in her professional interests; given her current audience. But that all changed when Mrs Bridie Boyle, nee Kelly, pounced on her from the school yard door.

For the erstwhile pupil Bridie, the sight of her snotty, tear-stained little dote being set upon by Iggy or her ilk must have been a clarion call to arms. But her eagerness to enter the affray with such vigour spoke of something deeper. Perhaps she saw a chance to even up old scores, to salve ancient schoolhouse wounds? Either way Iggy was in trouble, and she knew it. The shoe was on the other foot now and baldy had it coming to her. Bridie loved a good scrap.

To call someone 'seven different types of bitches' is a sort of an Irish catch-all encompassing the many insults one woman can heap upon another without actually getting herself arrested by the Guards. I'd be lying if I said I could remember every slur that was cast between the crimson-faced holy sister and her ex-pupil in those first few seconds. 'Whore of nun' definitely featured, and I'm almost certain the word 'hallion' was bandied about in the now blue air. If the case had gone to court, which nowadays it almost certainly would, I'd have made a poor witness for either side. Even though I'd heard most of the words before (I was the youngest of six) I would have been hard pushed to truthfully swear who said what to whom, such was the melee. I must admit though 'baldy 'oul bitch' was new.

Whipping her wailing baby up in one ham hock of an arm and catching the edge of the now threadbare veil with the other, the Mammy, rather than pulling at the garment, wound it tightly around her spare ham hock, thus drawing the now cowering nun into her considerable body space. Eye to eye, the Mammy then loudly informed the Mother that if she ever 'even looked crooked' at a child of hers again her husband Ger The Mechanic would come calling. Striding towards the blue door, a smirking Cepta straddling her hip, she turned back to the nun with a final shot across the bows.

"You've had your warning! And you can say goodbye to

My Ger mending your manky Morris Minor from now on."

The quivering nun went to take after Bridie, when she was suddenly distracted. A human eruption rocked the drill hall. One of the frail little townies, who was doubtless nervous even before witnessing the violence, gurgled a Vesuvius of vomit into the gaberdine hood of the girl sitting on the floor in front of her. Could this day get any better? Jacinta Healy (the vomiter) and Catherine Early (the vomitee) began to wail in unison. The nun changed course and ran towards the drill hall, reluctantly relinquishing the chase.

Things quietened down considerably after that, as the new intake of Low Babies, as we were known, was shepherded swiftly to the relative calm of the lovely Miss Gargan's classroom.

At the end of this exhilarating first foray into the world, Mammy met me at the school gate at two o'clock, and we strolled the country mile home together. Back in sixties Ireland, no one wished you a nice day or asked you if you had one. That was for Yanks. And since every day was the same it would have been a waste of words. My Mam, like all the others, was not particularly curious whether her youngest had enjoyed the day or otherwise. Irish Mammies had plenty of questions, of course they did. But they wanted facts, not feelings.

"Did you eat all your sandwiches?"

"Yes."

"And your apple?"

"Yes."

That wasn't a complete lie, since I'd taken a couple of bites out of it before firing it into the ditch of whitethorn hedges around the schoolyard. Everyone knew that you needed two hands to play Red Rover and I was keen to play with the big girls in High Babies – the year above us. It's not that I didn't have older girls in my life, I had two older sisters, and plethora of cousins. But some of these big girls wore store-bought navy uniforms, unlike the awful homemade hand me downs foisted on me. These girls from the town had shop bread followed by Mars bars for lunch! These were the girls I needed to know. I'd overheard enough heated debates at home to know that the chance of Mammy changing my lunch menu to include such delicacies was nil. Despite pleas from older brothers and sisters, cheese or ham on homemade brown bread would be my lot for many a year to come. There was nothing I could do about the brown bread, but the town girls didn't need to see my homegrown apple, which if Mammy had anything about her, would have been swapped out for a Crunchie.

Later that evening, as Daddy allowed me to help him fill his after-dinner pipe, he asked me what I thought of school. Like most four-year-olds I was an assiduous little vocabulary builder and had spent no small part of my toddler years with Mammy quietly listening to her chat with other Mammies. Unsurprisingly the conversations were often around childbirth and the various activities and discomforts which ensued, more of this later. Daddy always enjoyed listening to me wrangle the English language. It gave him no end of fun to hear phrases like 'the lair cheg of the table' or 'lowing the mawn'. So when he was in the mood, Daddy would sit me up for what I called a 'chatter.' These spoonerisms, of which of course I was unaware, caused no end of laughter from visiting uncles, aunts, and neighbours. Remember there was no television, and of course I was delighted to bask in the warmth of adult attention.

For the most part I usually made myself perfectly understood while doing considerable damage to the spoken word. But there were occasions when my tentative grasp on the true meaning of words sort of slipped between two stools. That evening, my after-dinner exchange over tea and plain biscuits (I was happy to chat, the biscuits were a bonus) probably threw up the starkest example of this. Over the years it's become so entrenched in family lore I'm almost proud of it.

In my defence, the fault for my linguistic shortcomings on this occasion lay partly with Mammy. Her two favourite maxims were 'You'll have me tearing my hair out' and 'Running around like a headless chicken." According to herself she engaged in one or other of these activities daily, often concurrently. Much like the 'seven different types of bitches' idiom these were handy catch-alls to vent the endless annoyance of mothering a large brood, who expected her to provide everything for them by way of domestic needs. In fact, although I've been one myself, the role of housewife and stay-at-home mother is, in truth, ludicrous. Life-giving, delightful, rewarding, but ludicrous.

Either way, Mammy's two phrases had confused me, and to be hairless was to be headless and vice versa. Everyone in Low Babies knew the nun's secret now. God's work must have been harder than housework. Because the smooth skulled nun had obviously torn all her hair out.

"Well. What did you think of school, pet?" Dad enquired.

"Good." I nodded my head. "Missive Garden said we're getting slates and chalk tomorrow to do our ABCs."

"Missive Garden?" He bit his lip and Mammy turned slightly from the kitchen sink.

"And what about the other girls in your class, are they nice?"

"Yep." I licked crumbs from my thumb and forefinger, wondering if I could venture back to the tin for a third biscuit. Mammy had returned to dishwashing, and Daddy, with his own sweet tooth, wouldn't dream of denying a child a treat.

"Did you play with them all?"

"Nope, I didn't play with Septic."

"Who?"

"Septic."

Daddy let out a roar of laughter, almost burning his hand as he caught the pipe falling from his open mouth.

"Who?" he boomed again as Mammy turned a second time from the kitchen sink grinning.

"A girl called Septic Boil. She had to go home early because her Mammy won tug-of-war with a headless nun. So, she didn't get to play with anyone.'

"What?" Mammy was pulling off the rubber gloves now.

"Mrs Boil came back and took Septic home with her."

"Did she now?" Mam gave Daddy a knowing look.

"Which nun?" Mam again.

"Sister Ingratious, and then she came into our class after lunch, and she said that Septic had made HailHolyMary very sad, and she never seen a girl in a Saint Milophena's umiform being such a shame on herself and her family and that if any of us did such sinful mishaviour or used such vulva words we could forget making our First Holy

Mecunion and would likely end up in the roaring fires of hell for all maternity."

I looked at them both as I finished imparting this solemn news. Poor Mammy was bent over clutching her tummy and holding on to the metal edge of the kitchen sink. Daddy, pipe discarded now, was wiping tears from his contorted face with his big brown farm hands. I was quite shocked at their response and thought to console them somewhat.

"But she had the black tablecloth back on her head, and she'd stopped making bubbles with her mouth," I offered kindly.

After several minutes of snorting (Daddy) and shrieking (Mammy) laughter, Dad put his forehead in his hands declaring, "Christ on a bike Bernie, what will we do with this one?"

What? Baby Jesus had a bike! Why didn't I know this? I needed to get to grips with my ABCs. Santa had an important letter coming.

**Maeve McGoohan**

## On rising

I wake at dawn to walk with the rising sun
as silence softens trees before birdsong —
I could chance upon a frog or any secret
hiding in density which may emerge clear
and strong like a thought from an uncluttered
mind passing wordlessly through space
and time. A windfall catching its breath in my
garden as pathways sway and intermingle.

A seep of dew lingers on leaves, brushes
my skirt to damp from ankle to thigh —
cool and clinging, whispering its odyssey
in tongues, ordering my thoughts into
couplets which will erupt onto the page
mysteriously at some stage but now my
fingers brush the dampness sparingly,
exchanging silent messages with plants.

Through the pathways I carve to better
ensconce myself in the midst of growth,
I slither almost silent while sun wakes day,
stems the mist, lightens the load, leaves
a halo here and there, to cap its playful
impact, pierce the shadows, enliven dull
spaces, maybe burn its message too deep,
scald shy tendrils into wither and wilt.

***Ann Simic***

## How to exist

Put on a big coat when it's cold,
take it off in the sunshine.
Balance your expectations
against those who mistrust you.
Feed the birds, finish the laundry.
Ponder those skeletons found
in Pompeii.
Develop delicate delineation dissertations,
remain aware of quiet inconsideration.
Speak poorly of yourself,
speak poorly of others.
Eat water crackers when nauseous in the dead of night,
eat water crackers on the streets of Paris.

Hold yourself to only the things you can manage,
aspire to manage more.
Never forget everything happened to happen
to bring your happenings here.
What miracles did you eat for breakfast?
How long do you have?
What's to show for the day?
Never lie when you say you love someone.
Never pass up the opportunity
to giggle in the snack aisle of the supermarket.

**Lucy Tomov**

## Bring me my ear trumpet!

Bring me my ear trumpet!
Bring me my cane!
Take me to the brink of death
but bring me back again.

Take my old leaking heart!
Take my wandering mind!
Bring me something whole and new
and take me somewhere kind.

Bring me my happy songs!
Bring me the blues!
Take me where the music plays
and sing me cheerful news.

### *Paul Downton*

Paul's pastel drawing 'Self-portrait of a Widower' was done as a way of expressing something that he found difficult to articulate after losing his wife, muse and partner of 46 years, Chérie Hoyle. The framed original was purchased by Peninsula Home Hospice and is now displayed in their Mornington HQ as an aid to that organisation's mission to help people navigate the often difficult and unfamiliar process of coming to terms with the end-of-life journeys of themselves and their loved ones. Paul wishes to personally, and gratefully, acknowledge the support of PHH during the crucial end-of-life and bereavement processes experienced by Chérie, their family, and himself.

# Belated birthday greetings

My maternal grandfather Jack brought his family to Australia in 1923 hoping to create opportunities for a better life away from the remnants of the wartorn city of London. Britain was struggling to rebuild, and Jack's cousin Joe who had moved to Melbourne some years before, had written telling him about this wonderful country untouched physically by the terrible First World War in Europe.

Jack had started a business in 1919 making prostheses for some of the thousands of damaged soldiers returning to Britain from the French and Belgian trenches with missing limbs. Joe told him many Australian servicemen had also arrived home in less than whole condition which meant he could continue his prostheses business there.

The family consisted of Jack, my grandmother Jane plus their two daughters, Raechel and Hannah. Their son Joe, (named after his father's cousin), had gone to America in 1922 *'to make his fortune.'*

They initially settled in the Melbourne suburb of Northcote but later on moved south of the city to the beachside suburb of Elwood. Jack initially presented some of his prosthetics to the hospital in Heidelberg where many of the badly injured soldiers were undergoing rehabilitation but found that there were already Australian companies supplying false limbs made from better materials. He then looked around for other business opportunities and finally bought an established dry cleaning company whilst Raechel and Hannah began making dresses for neighbourhood ladies.

ଈଈଈ

Jack found that operating a business in Australia was less complicated than in England and despite the worldwide recession of the early 1930s he managed to keep the company afloat. As Europe once again slipped into war footing and tens of thousands of young Aussies signed up to fight alongside the British, dry cleaning of army uniforms became a major part of the business. There were plenty of older men and women looking for work and my father who had met and married Hannah in 1930, gave up making furniture with his brother and took over the manager's role at the dry cleaning company to take pressure off my aging grandfather.

Throughout the long war, Jack's brother Harry remained in England operating a number of successful businesses including cinemas, live theatres and amusement parks in towns north of London. Somehow they were not targeted by the Germans as the area was not industrial and despite the war, people still wanted to be entertained. Going to the cinema was especially popular as the newsreels which were screened before the movies kept everyone abreast of the events in Europe and later on, the expanded war encompassing the Pacific Ocean region.

People living in the southern cities such as Melbourne, Adelaide and Hobart believed they were too far away from the action for Japanese aircraft to reach them. In actual fact, it was only some decades later that they heard that the Japanese managed to fly some reconnaissance planes over Melbourne searching for the American officers' base which was located in Port Melbourne.

After the end of the war, my grandfather tried to convince his brother to migrate to the 'lucky country.' Darwin had suffered heavy bombardment by the Japanese whilst the rest of this vast land escaped virtually unscathed.

The two brothers remained in contact by writing letters, usually at least once per month. Birthday and anniversary cards became a tradition between the two families and if one of these celebrations was accidentally missed, the culprit would receive a chastising from the other.

This was the situation that occurred in March 1954:

Harry's 50$^{th}$ birthday was 25$^{th}$ March and Jack bought a card that featured a photo of a Melbourne tram with the number 50 showing as its route number. He wrote inside about how good it would be if Harry would reconsider and bring his family out to Melbourne so they could celebrate these occasions together face to face.

He took the card to the post office and asked if the price had changed for airmail to England since he last sent a card to his brother's wife. He remembered that it had been one shilling and sixpence.

He was told that the British airline BOAC that carries huge amount of mail between the two countries had recently placed the latest Constellation aircraft into service and it was proving to be faster and more efficient. The price for airmailing a greeting card had increased to one shilling and nine pence. 'We believe the mail can now be delivered anywhere in Britain six days after it is posted in Sydney and eight` days when posted in Melbourne,' the clerk told him. As it was the 11$^{th}$ of March when Jack handed over the money and the relevant stamps stuck on the envelope he departed the post office believing the card would be delivered in plenty of time for Harry's birthday.

Neither Jack nor the post office clerk could have foreseen what happened next.

The *Sydney Morning Herald* headline on 14th March 1954 read:

## BOAC LOCKHEED CONSTELLATION CRASH.
## BIG DEATH-ROLL IN BLAZING WRECK
### SINGAPORE Saturday (A.A.P.-Reuters)

*A BOAC Constellation airliner flying from Sydney to London crashed at Singapore this afternoon and burst into flames.*

*Of 40 people on board, (31 passengers and a crew of nine) only eight are believed to have survived. All were members of the crew. (Qantas authorities in Sydney this morning released the names of three Sydney victims of the crash.)*

*The airliner came in to land at Kallang Airport (seven miles from Singapore), but after touching down it blew up behind a wall of orange flames. A brisk wind fanned the blaze and black smoke curled to 1000 feet.*

*Horrified eye witnesses, including friends and relatives of some of those aboard, said they saw only one of the plane's retractable wheels come down as the Constellation approached.*

*One said that he heard two explosions as the plane hit the ground . . .*

The newspaper report continued for many more paragraphs but I believe I have shown enough for the reader to appreciate the serious damage that resulted from the crash. After investigation by the authorities it was determined that the flight crew was over-tired and may have brought the plane in too low and too fast resulting in the wheels clipping a brick wall at the end of the runway.

The plane hit the runway at an awkward angle causing it to roll over with the nose section splitting apart spilling the crew onto the tarmac. The rest of the plane exploded and became engulfed in flames. There was no hope of saving the passengers.

My grandfather had no idea when he read about the plane crash in Singapore that his birthday card to his brother was on that flight. As time passed he wondered why Harry hadn't written to say thanks for the card.

Some weeks after all passenger remains had been removed and investigators had completed their gruesome tasks, the wreckage was cleared to be disposed of. A final search incredibly discovered one of the many items in the burnt out cargo hold turned out to have escaped being completely incinerated . . . it was a heavy canvas Royal Mail post office sack full to the top with mail destined for England.

Some of the letters were singed beyond recognition but a small number including my grandfather's birthday card with the clearly addressed envelope was sent on their merry way. Harry eventually received his brother's greeting approximately six weeks after his birthday!

There is a saying that despite all obstacles, the mail must get through and this was an amazing example of the Post Office's dedication.

Post script: Some years later, Harry did bring his family to Australia and introduced Australians to drinking coffee made on the first imported Gaggia espresso coffee machine when he opened a café called Il Cappuccino in Fitzroy St. Kilda.

***John Aarons***

## People

Some people look sad, some look worried, some are angry, wanting to hurt others
Most do not know how to discipline their mind, some think that is not a problem
To discipline their impulses and certain behavior and minds
Many people have been influenced by almost anything or anyone
I choose to gain knowledge from the smarter and wiser ones
This is what I have had to learn and this is what I have chosen to learn
It is a way I have learnt to survive and cope in this world of many people
I have silently questioned their motives and how they choose to think the way they do
For many people in this world are a bit broken and have lost their way
I know they need to find themselves again
When the time is right for them
Takes courage to look at things about oneself that we don't share with others
Sometimes we even hide it from ourselves
Many positive benefits that one gains along the way
When we know what is hidden
Many tools in my bag now that have helped me so, always a book or two and insights of the secrets and knowledge from the great ones
Carl Jung, Buddha and other great Masters
It has proven to be right
It has worked for me
I would rather listen to more knowledgeable ones
The wiser and smarter ones

***Rose Lumbaca Crane***

# I for Isabel

Isabel was worried. She missed one period, but now she'd missed another. But missing a second period was a different matter, She could be pregnant, she thought with alarm. But why? When she'd taken every precaution before she and Henry had sex. It was then the words of the obstetrician had come to her. Ninety per cent safe, he had said, handing the small plastic object to her. Had one of Henry's sperms managed to break free and fertilize one of her eggs?

She didn't want a baby, not yet. Not until she had become used to living with Henry. She'd found living with him difficult. It was one thing to enjoy his company while dating him, but another to having to adjust to his ways and especially since he was a minister of the church.

She felt that Henry was expecting too much of her. Why, only last Sunday, he'd put pressure on her to attend the afternoon service when she'd already attended the morning one. She'd only gone along to please him but had found the experience distasteful. Most of the congregation, such as they were, were sound asleep in their pews. No, it was the last time she would attend the afternoon service. In fact, she'd already made up her mind that she would attend church once a day despite Henry's admonitions.

That evening she broached the subject.

'I think I'm pregnant,' she said nervously.

'You're what?'

'You heard what I said.' She burst into tears. 'I don't want a baby.'

'I don't want one either,' Henry said. 'It's far too soon. Whatever will the congregation say?'

'Is that what you're worried about, Henry? I thought you'd be concerned at how I feel about having a baby.'

Henry looked abashed. 'I'm sorry Isabel. I have a lot on my mind. There is much to be done – the visiting of parishioners, the preparation of services, the attending of meetings and being available for those who need help. Once I fit into the role, I'd be happy to have a baby. However, if you think you're pregnant, I suggest you see Dr. Paul.'

'I don't want to see Dr. Paul. I'd prefer Dr. Turner. He's more my age.'

'But Dr. Paul is Presbyterian,' Henry said.

'Presbyterian or Methodist. What does it matter, so long as I am happy with the doctor I choose.'

It did matter to Henry. Dr. Paul was an elder of the church and he didn't want to offend him.

**Lorraine Doney**

# Senior love

In a quiet part of the Swiss forest nestled beside a small frozen lake there was a secret little place for sauna lovers.
Only local people were allowed to visit this place.
But for them it was an exception.
They were visiting their retired Swiss friends who they met a while ago on a cruise.
Margrith held her towel tightly around her perfectly-shaped hourglass figure,
which she had kept in her senior years.
She glanced at her husband and gave a shy smile.
"I haven't done this before," she whispered
"Me neither," he said in a baritone voice.
"So let's have some fun, trying new things together," Michael said.
Inside they sat on a warm wooden bench, getting slowly used to the heat.
Inhaling deeply the fragrance scent of the Swiss forest.
Both felt the heat on their bodies
which started them sweating in a way they had never experienced before.
They smiled at each other and gave a quick kiss on the lips.
She leaned her head against his shoulder
and felt her heart beating in time with his.
Through the window they could see soft white flakes of snow falling.

> Margrith said spontaneously "Let's make this a habit" Michael nodded, took her hand and said, "Every Thursday afternoon."

In the pine-thinned slope above the lake there was a hut that people whispered about rather than posted. It belonged, in the way small local things belong, to no one in particular and to everyone who had been trusted with the directions. A path – narrow, salted in winter, lined with birch skeletons – led to a door that creaked the same two notes every time you opened it. Inside, the air remembered heat.

Margrith and Michael had come by train and bus and then by foot, the kind of arrival that collected a few small complications and made them feel earned. They carried nothing but towels and the polite, careful curiosity of long acquaintances turned friends – retired colleagues of the sea, people you met on a river and kept meeting in the margins of life. The hut sat at the lip of the frozen lake, a low building, rough-hewn and soft with years. A grey cloud lay low over the water. Snow had been falling for hours; the world outside the little window was muffled, as if someone had chosen to lay cotton over the edges of the day.

Margrith tightened the towel around her and laughed quietly at how attentive she still was to appearances. In the mirror of the small prep room she saw her own profile: forehead, the soft slope of cheekbones, a mouth that still knew how to decide. The years had given her lines but not a diminished appetite for small pleasures. Michael, taller, with a face that had kept its blunt honesty, moved with the slow economy of someone who had learned not to hurry. They were both older in the way that makes knees complain and memory shine, the kind of older where you begin measuring life by the acquaintances you keep rather than the projects you start.

They had met once on a cruise – one evening over coffee and a conversation about the loneliness of ports – and had found, in the soft logic of chance, a kind of friendship that asked for nothing dramatic and gave everything comfortable. In the months since, they exchanged letters and short messages that contained more of themselves than the messages warranted. This afternoon felt like a natural next step, a test of the old and the new.

The sauna smelled of cedar and old steam. The bench was warm beneath them; the room felt like a palm cupped to the heat. They sat with towels folded at their hips, shoulders scarcely apart. The heat was not theatrical; it rose modestly, the way good things do, and let them settle into it. As the temperature climbed, the body's map rearranged itself: memories compressed, breath lengthened, the small inventory of aches and grievances smoothed by the slow hand of warmth.

Snow traced a slow pattern across the window; each flake was a small forgiveness. Margrith closed her eyes and listened to the sound of the wood as it sighed and released. Beside her, Michael's breathing was even, the low cadence of someone who could still measure silence. There was a moment when they simply sat – no speaking, only an exchange of presence – and the hut felt full of a gentle complicity.

"I haven't done this before," Margrith said, as if reminding herself, not him.

"Me neither." His answer was a quiet fact, like a small book placed on the table.

So they did not perform bravery. They allowed curiosity to be enough.

The heat made their skins feel friendlier to their own hands. A strip of gold sunlight – thin as a coin – found the window and drew a patch of light on the bench. Margrith turned and looked at Michael, and the look held no sharpness: only an astonishment at being here, at the simple competence of being wanted. She leaned against his shoulder as you lean against a lifetime's later chapter, and there was no pretence in the contact – no theatre of passion, only the honest, plain language of two bodies saying yes to warmth.

They spoke in fragments: about the way the lake had once thawed early when they were young, about a book Michael had read years ago and could not recall the end of, about a niece who had taken up pottery in the city. Their voices floated between one another like paper boats on a slow current. Occasionally they would catch each other's hands, and each time the contact was brief and exact, like the punctuation to a sentence.

When the heat made the edges of their thoughts soft, Margrith reached out and pressed the heel of her hand lightly against the small of Michael's back. He turned, and they shared a kiss that had everything a kiss needed: given slowly, returned carefully, the small talk of lips that had learned to save exuberance for other moments. It landed somewhere without fanfare – sufficient, true.

Outside the window the snow thickened. The world beyond the glass was the colour and texture of a memory: softened, distant, kindly. Inside, their breathing became a steady tide, and the sauna's wood took witness.

Later, after stepping into the brisk air and feeling the shock that makes you feel more alive than any grand gesture, they wrapped themselves in towels and walked to the lake's edge. The ice lay flat and brittle; their footprints were temporary registrations against a white field. They did not undress to plunge or shout; they stayed with it – an economy of gestures that felt, in itself, intimate.

Margrith found an ordinary stone and picked it up, warmed by the sunless day. She turned it over in her palm and said, almost to herself, "We should do this more often."

Michael looked at her with the kind of look that understands proposals and promises are not always the same. "Every Thursday?" he offered, lightly. The suggestion was both the joke and the anchor. He would say the day precisely, and she would hear its rhythm.

She nodded, the motion small, satisfactory. "Every Thursday," she repeated, and the syllables made it sound like a calendar being softly taped into place. There was a humour in choosing something so mundanely specific; there was also a courage in it. A habit, after all, is a humble kind of fidelity.

They walked back toward the hut, steps soundless on salt and snow. In the hut's vestibule they shared a thermos of strong tea, and their hands met over the cup as the warmth passed from vessel to palm to palm. The ritual of ordinary things – tea, towels, the quietness of exchanged glances – felt, for the first time in a long while, like a reclamation of small joys.

Months later, the Thursdays took on shape. They met not because love had become a thunderclap, but because a space had opened in the week that belonged to them. Sometimes they argued gently about trivialities, sometimes they read aloud to one another from a book they were both pretending to like. They brought friends sometimes, sat in the company of others who appreciated the hut's unadvertised grace. At other times they came alone and held the habit like a small, nourishing secret.

The promise of Thursday was not a guarantee against sorrow – life remained as it had been, with its frayed edges and sudden small griefs. But the practice of warmth, the steady appointment with simple pleasure, made the rest of their days softer at the edges. They learned that affection could be a slow-building architecture: benches and steam, a thermos and a shared word, a fortnight of snow and a thin coin of sunlight across a wooden seat.

In the end, the hut kept what it always had – heat and wood and a small window that framed snow. What changed was their attendance: two names on an unspoken list. The ritual they made together was modest, and modesty suited them. It let them be present without theatrics, close without needing to prove anything. And when, years later, the town's bus stopped running past their street and other conveniences shifted, they still had their Thursdays: a line drawn gently across the calendar that said, in simple, unadorned language, here is warmth, here is company, here is a promise.

***Monika Nuesch***

## Why poetry

Poetry removes the mask.
It is raw. Unfiltered.
It is a shedding of armour
worn out by too many internal battles.
It is chipping at solid walls
made of bricks laid
at various lifetime events.

It is human nature to tuck away
what lays hidden in silence . . .
Fear. Fault. Grief.
Guilt. Blame. Shame.
Temptation. Lies. Deceit.
Regrets. Rejection. Abandonment.
Doubt. Weakness. Mistakes.
Hurt. Heartbreak. Pain.
We inflict on ourselves.
We inflict on others.

It is an incredible burden we try to offload.
But passed back because it is ours to bear.
It gets consumed. Then regurgitated.
Over and over.
Or buried. Some shallow graves.
Some deep in dirt.
All of it hiding in the dark.

The weight of all these thoughts
wrapped tightly around the soul
sacredly unravels in poetry.
Turned inside out – to touch the light.

Poetry removes shards.
It is messy. Unpredictable.
Sometimes it bleeds emotions endlessly.
It leaves you exhausted. Weak.
Sometimes it is superficial.
Like a splinter with very little damage.
But a relief to release nonetheless.

Poetry is courage.
It speaks what the voice dare not utter.
It is like a whispered prayer.
Please absolve me. Give me grace.
Then lay it to rest in a safe sanctuary.
Let the wounds heal
without temptation to pick at the scars.

***Aileen Heal***

# Five minutes of fame

*This is an excerpt from a book dedicated to Mark Robinson, written by Caroline McCrindle, and told as if Mark is telling the story himself.*

The Mornington Peninsula is rich in history and natural beauty. Long before European settlement, the Bunurong people roamed its coastline, gathering shellfish and hunting kangaroo and possum. Today, I drive the same lands to work – Cape Schanck Road, where kangaroos still leap across unexpectedly.

Portsea, named by settler James Ford in the 1840s, grew to fame with its pier, cypress trees, and the grand Delgany mansion. Built in 1925 by Harold Armytage, Delgany overlooked both Port Phillip Bay and Bass Strait. It later served as a WWII army hospital and a school for the deaf run by the Dominican Sisters. Portsea is also remembered for the 1967 disappearance of Prime Minister Harold Holt at Cheviot Beach – just two months after I was born in Watsonia.

Watsonia was quiet, close-knit, and safe. I remember walks to Kalparrin Gardens to feed the ducks and trips to the local IGA with Mum. In 1980, our family moved to Tootgarook on the Peninsula. It was all empty blocks and open space – perfect for flying kites on fishing rods. I collected bottles for pocket money and earned the nickname "Excuse Me" for my polite persistence.

A near-drowning at Rye Beach scarred me early, and soon after, a bike accident left spokes embedded in my foot. Accident-prone from the start, I once even broke a friend's neck by sleepily stepping on it. My teenage years were tough but formative. We couldn't afford much—certainly not the $5,000 for a block of land. I worked hard for every cent: paper rounds, bingo cans, even walking to work from Rosebud to Portsea when my bike was stolen.

In 1986, I landed my first real job at Delgany Country House Hotel. I worked long hours, sometimes on just three hours' sleep between shifts at Delgany and Sorrento Bakery. I eventually stayed 13 years, learning seafood prep under master chef Herman Schneider, who turned the old deaf school into a celebrated restaurant. Later, I worked for John Rubira, another seafood maestro.

Then came the big moment that changed everything: a radio and a dream.

**Big dreams fly high**

It was 1992, and I was blasting music in the garage, tuned to my favourite station, Fox FM 101.9. That jingle, "In the summertime when the weather is fine, turn your stereo up to 101.9," stuck in my head. Right then and there, I had the idea: personalised numberplates.

The first option – "FOX ME" – cracked up my brother with its unintended double meaning. So I pivoted to the ultimate choice: FM1019. Surely the station already owned it, I thought. But I had nothing to lose.

At the tiny VicRoads office in Dromana, I applied. The lady at the counter smiled, checked her computer, and said, "You'll need permission from Fox FM's manager." She handed me a number.

I called D'Rock at Fox FM. He asked for time to consider.

Weeks passed. I called again. He said, "I don't see why not." That was it – I owned FM1019.

When I finally picked up the glossy black-and-white plates, I was over the moon. I sent my car, a yellow TE Cortina, up to Mirboo North, where a mate's brother gave it a fresh coat of paint. It sparkled. She was my pride and joy.

## A life in motion

By then, I was an experienced kitchenhand and keen driver. My Cortina meant freedom. I advanced quickly from Ls to Ps and explored work all over the Peninsula.

I loved Fox FM. I was obsessed. Every car I had since wore those plates. I collected memorabilia, followed the DJs, and kept the dream alive: to one day meet Hamish Blake and Andy Lee, Fox FM's iconic duo.

Over the years, I'd call in to their shows, leave messages, enter competitions; anything to get noticed. I even dreamed of handing over my plates to them, believing they'd appreciate their significance. I never gave up.

## Five minutes of fame

Finally, the day came. Fox FM was holding a meet-and-greet. I drove up with my partner, armed with memorabilia and the numberplates. We waited in line, hearts pounding.

When I met Hamish and Andy, I was overwhelmed. They were warm, funny, and genuinely interested in my story. I explained how long I'd had the plates and how much their show meant to me. I offered them the plates, but they declined, saying I was their biggest fan and should keep them.

It was surreal. Just two ordinary people from the Mornington Peninsula, standing face-to-face with our radio heroes. My five minutes of fame.

❧❧❧

Today, those plates still mean everything to me. They represent persistence, nostalgia, identity, and a little bit of magic. My journey wasn't glamorous, but it was real – fuelled by hard work, humble dreams, and a love for music and radio.

Sometimes the smallest things – a song on the radio, a bike ride to work, or a personalised plate – can carry the biggest dreams.

*Caroline McCrindle*

## This tower

Shuffling triumph and disaster, your structure, etherborne, dressed in finery, spears the moon like a violin.

Your walls wrapped in rhythm — music, song, voices that echo your summit; alone, free in a crowd of bohemian elegance.

Dance your oaken floor, vibrate your history, arches, motifs, scrolls, classic cornices — heritage assured.

A century and some since your birth in 1866 — a building boom when dire deeds were done to people in their own land —

that sorry story written on your reluctant watch, within your secret walls, revealed to those who listen in night's silence.

You housed many — land office to post office, vital, ordinary tasks, orchestrated in your stately space of Corinthian columns.

High Renaissance, the apogee, the crescendo, rising to more on the following floor, topped by the tower — octagonal, rare.

I lived with you here over three raging years, here, with those I love. Set you up for music, poetry, dance, drama, art, food, drink —

packed to the rafters each day and night, you encircled me, embraced me as we bloomed sleepless, until time ticked towards goodbye.

Now, thirty years on, you and I persist separately but recently I steamed up the highway to you, where music of my progeny lit your being.

The overflowing crowd drank the rich brew of all of you, linked, arm-in-arm, with art, surging to your summit singly and in unison.

**Ann Simic**

## Look at me

I used to be a glacier
Now look at me

I used to be a glacier
That made its way down to the sea
Look at me

I used to be a glacier
That made its way down to the sea
And slowly over centuries
Set baby glaciers free
Look at me

I used to be a glacier
Now drink me

**Paul Downton**

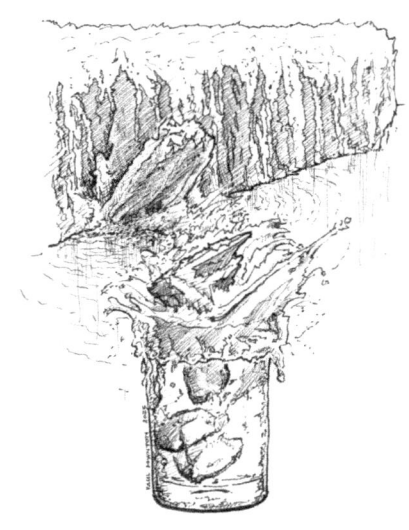

# Local transport- Indian style

The casual tourist to India often doesn't get a chance to live like the locals, often ferried around by air-conditioned taxi or tourist bus. Needing to see more of the area I was living in, I decided to catch the local bus to Mapusa (pronounced Mapsa for some strange reason) where there was the usual Friday market day.

I waited patiently at the gateway of the old Portuguese house that I was staying in, hoping that eventually a bus would pass by. There are no timetables and even asking a local about bus times leads to a puzzled look and a "yes, yes" and a wobble of the head response which could mean anything from "I have no idea what this foreigner is saying", to "I don't want to lose face so I will say what she wants to hear." Nothing is straightforward or clear about India.

My eyes scanned the road, I tried to muster the patience of the traveller and every so often had to shake my head from side to side to indicate to a tuk-tuk driver who had slowed down as he approached me, that I didn't want a lift. I was being independent and capable I told myself. The drivers probably just thought I was a mad middle-aged Westerner.

The day was warming up, the sky the usual pale blue, the palm trees swaying along the side of the dusty road, the traffic of scooters whizzed past all loaded with multiple occupants, most on their mobile phone. But my patience paid off and the rickety bus arrived, painted various shades of blue and yellow, looking like a relic from World War II, all metal and lacking padding. I hailed it down, feeling very chuffed at myself and clambered aboard. Luckily it wasn't too crowded and I found a seat, then handed over my ten rupee note for the fare – twenty cents in Aussie money, and then settled back to watch the passing scenery. I remembered a good deal of the major sights from my last visit and practised trying to memorise new landmarks, for you never know when you could get lost.

All along the road there were brightly coloured houses, purple and pink favoured this year with trimmings in white, or small, makeshift roadside eateries, selling anything from omelettes to freshly squeezed cane sugar drinks. The bus route then travelled through open fields of vegetables and the remains of rice crops, before lurching us into the mayhem of the town roundabout where it was best to close one's eyes and pray to whatever god was in favour that day. I leaped off the bus, a spring in my step, glad to be alive.

Being Friday, the market was full of locals going about their business, buying for the family. There were avenues of stalls selling lady finger bananas, piles of ruby red pomegranates, black grapes and green custard apples. Other aisles specialised in fabrics and lengths of sari material, all vivid colours and edged in sequins. I found myself favouring the bright colours and wondering what I could buy that wouldn't look too out of place in downtown Glen Waverley. Everything, I sighed and focussed on buying the fruit I wanted, ripe figs, lychees and bananas. All the stall holders vied for customers, handing over samples of their fruit. You would never need to go hungry here.

I spent the next hour wandering the market, taking in the frantic pace of life and the sheer numbers of people, all intent on their chores. A man sitting on the corner of the market area fixed the handle of my hand bag, broken by loading far too many items into it before getting on the plane. There were other men near him also fixing shoes, resoling them and mending what they could. There is a sense that nothing is wasted here, that the modern throwaway culture of home has still to hit this southern part of India.

I treated myself to a stop for lunch at a café in the middle of the market area. They made wonderful meat samosas and banana lassi to die for. The décor was 1960s laminex tables and overhead ceiling fans and a menu with spelling mistakes galore, but who cared.

I knew where the bus had stopped so I eventually headed back there. It is not what I would describe as a bus terminal as such, more like a sea of confusion with buses coming and going at seemingly random intervals and times, all vying with each other to move and park and disgorge their contents. There are no signs up or designated areas to wait just a wave of the hand to the left or the right as I asked where the bus to Anjuna would be. Patience again was needed.

Finally, a young girl took pity on me and waved that I should follow her to a bus that had just arrived. Hardly had the bus stopped and the people flowed out than the rest of us moved as one into the now crowded bus. I stood, realising that this was to be my lot returning home. No seat for the foreigner and no seat for the middle-aged or even elderly among us. The young men had firmly laid claim to their seat and felt no shame. We stood for ten minutes or so, the bus filling up with more people than I could have ever thought would fit. There must have been 80 or so people crammed in. My sense of personal space had evaporated in the first minute, my armpit, fortunately shaved and with deodorant, firmly in the face of the passenger next to me.

And someone else's leg squashed up against my thigh. A young man started to chat. "What did I have in my bags? Where was I staying?", all asked with curious interest and a certain naiveté. I took no offense as none was meant. I put my shopping bags up on the rack and hung on. The sweat began to run as trickles down my back and I longed for the bus to move so that at least some air flow would happen.

I got my wish and we chugged out of the depot, the engine whining slightly under the weight of all of us and the gears mashing ever so slightly. We lumbered along at first and then as we headed out toward the more open countryside, the driver put his foot down. We sped, we swayed. We lurched precariously from side to side and I had flashes of fictitious headlines in papers back home: *Overloaded bus crashes down embankment. One foreigner dead.* But still we kept on, stopping occasionally, picking up even more passengers, with no one leaving. How many people can you fit in one bus I thought?

Finally, I came to an area I recognized as near my house. I yelled to the conductor. He had spent all his time hanging out of the bus and whistling a series of intricate messages to the driver when people needed to get off. The young conductor took my now squashed bags and helped me squeeze past the other occupants. No one was cross, no one complained, all stoically accepted this bus ride and closeness as part of everyday life. I emerged from the bus, light-hearted and light-headed and smiling and waved good bye to my fellow travellers.

My figs were warm and only slightly squashed but tasted magnificent.

**Di Motton**

## A love letter

Your cheeks in the cold
are a kind of pinkish red.
Blushing softened hues
below eyes of deeper blue.
I go with you
wherever the light splays out;
zebra stripes are
catching tight delights.
They're elongated, ephemeral,
roaming existential digressions.
In those seconds
my bliss gets to sing.
Its overture
merely confession,
your palm home
to a curled-over thing.
See, you pull out of me
many a small vice:
gossip over dinner,
break-neck speeds over yonder,
happy tears over toughness,
selfish questions over sonder.
You can like this you say
and I'll shake my head in fright.
But when I'm to your left,
you're always right.

**Lucy Tomov**

## Can a cafe be like a friend ?

Is being at your favorite cafe like catching up with a truly trusted friend? Studying, writing our ideas, hopes and dreams.
Feelings and thoughts on paper and what is going on in your life
Trying to figure out what happened, who said what and how I think and feel about it all
Sitting at a cafe, people watching, observing people, what one senses in people
All without worries about the consequences of what was spoken to another
The safety and haven of your favourite cafe
Seen as a middle ground where people meet Taking in the ambience, the friendliness of the staff
So many cafes to choose, which one to go for coffee today? The simple, retro look from the 50s, one of the first cafes
The Italians knew how to make a good coffee and food and still do
The owner of a cafe loved by many,
a man that was killed by a troubled man
People still go into the cafe and mention him and their experiences
They look forward to going to Pellegrini's when in town
Just some of the many cafes for people to meet in the middle ground to dream,
communicate and have a coffee or tea

*Rose Lumbaca Crane*

## Skeletons (σκελετοί)

It wasn't Jessica's favorite Greek restaurant, but since the majority of her colleagues loved it, and she wanted to join in the ritual Friday after-work meal, she didn't demur. The food there just never seemed like the real thing; nothing like what her mother cooked (when she could be bothered getting in touch with her "Greekness").

"Table booked for three, under the name of Paul." He announced their arrival confidently, almost with a sense of proprietorship. He was cute, Jessica thought, but always exuded a vague air of smug superiority, as if her knew it all.

The maître d ushered the little group to a table at the rear of the restaurant. They were all in good spirits, chattering excitedly. It had been a good day. They'd had a breakthrough in progress with one of the rheumatoid arthritis drugs.

After perusing the menu each revealed what took their fancy.

"Love the dips," declared Regan to the waiter. "Let's have the tadzeek, the bubbyganash, and a pile of pita for entrée."

"It's pronounced *tzadziki* and the Greeks don't call it babaganoush – it's *melitzanosalata*." Jessica couldn't help herself. She hated it when Aussies mispronounced foreign words.

Paul eyed her with a mocking smile. "Oh, little Miss Greek – you haven't even been there! How come?"

He didn't bother to wait for her answer, before launching into one of his interminable talks on all the wonderful places he had visited in Greece on his last vacation.

"Well of course Mykonos used to be the island for the rich and famous, but now it's got some competition from Antiparos and Santorini. I've got to say I prefer Corfu. Plenty of good British pubs there!"

"Why on earth would you go to Greece for British pubs!" Jess burst out.

"Why on earth have you never even been there? Your family is Greek, aren't they?" responded Paul. The whole group looked at her expectantly, so she decided an honest answer could be the best course of action.

"My mum left when she was young. She's never been very encouraging of me to go there I'm afraid. I think she had some bad stuff happen in her childhood, and she sort of wants to forget she even has any family over there."

"Well I think we should all take leave at the same time, and have a group trip there. It'd be ace!" announced Regan.

"That idea has legs. Tour leader at your disposal!" laughed Paul.

The mound of pita, with the not-so-generous plates of dip arrived, and eating overtook conversation.

৵৵৵

Jess always looked forward to Saturday breakfast with her mother. It was odd to be a working girl and still living at home, but hey, what young adults could afford their own home these days?

They sat together over yoghurt, fruit and scrambled eggs. Sally seemed unusually quiet.

"What's up Mum?"

"An email arrived from my sister. She tells me our mother is very ill, maybe even dying. She's begging me to come over and see her."

"So? You've never been back, and maybe now's the time."

Sally shook her head vigorously. "No way I'm going to see that woman. She ruined my childhood!"

"Mum, you always say this, but you never tell me exactly what happened. It can't have been that bad. Maybe somewhere along the line you have to forgive."

"You don't know anything!" her mother snapped. "I won't ever forgive her, and can we just leave this subject once and for all."

ۍۍۍ

"You are not going to believe this!" Paul's eyes positively shone as he addressed the Friday night dinner gathering. "You know what we were talking about – going to Greece together – well Dr Papadopoulos wants to team up with the Biomed Research organization in Athens. They are hosting some sort of international conference. The doc thinks we could learn a great deal by tagging along. We'd have to use part of our annual leave of course. We could do the work part then hit some islands and chill out."

Jessica felt her heart leap in her chest. Talk about a quirky twist of fate, good timing, or however you wanted to see it. I could finally meet my grandmother, thought Jess. Talk with my aunt Roula. Find out what the hell happened to my mother to make her so bitter and resentful.

It had been two months since Sally had received the email from her sister Afrodite. Roula, as she was called, had taken leave from her job in America to go to Greece. She'd been staying for a couple of weeks now with her sick mother, who, despite being rumoured to be on death's door, seemed to be hanging in to the bitter end.

The trouble was, the conference was in Athens and Jess's grandmother, Fotoula, lived way up in the north-west of the country. Jess would have to use all her annual leave for this one.

*ૡૡૡ*

The conference had been a roaring success. Biomedical researchers from all over the world had converged on Athens, sharing research papers, new ideas, and conviviality.

The old part of Athens, known as Plaka, was definitely the place to go for lively tavernas and nightlife. Each night they had recovered from an arduous day of ideas, learning and mingling, downing ouzo and discussing where they would head off to for the last days of their trip. Paul's vote for Corfu was overridden by the women, and since flights were relatively cheap and quicker than ferries, they all boarded an Aegean Airlines flight for Santorini.

Jess couldn't help but be awestruck by the first glimpse of the whitewashed town of Fira, strung out precariously along a ridge, overlooking the caldera, an expanse of azure water left after a massive volcanic eruption that destroyed many ancient societies. Blue-domed churches abounded, and the narrow cobbled alleyways were home to an endless string of restaurants, and shops sporting jewellery and souvenirs.

Each evening Paul led the group to the most touristy overpriced restaurant he could find, sitting with roving eyes on the lookout for vacationing celebrities. Then, together, the trio would amble along, in and out of shops, where Paul and Regan, but not Jess, forked out euros on gold and silver, rubies and onyx, and imitation museum antiquities. It was a tourist paradise, and money seemed to be the ruling deity.

Despite the island's beauty Jess was relieved to part ways with her colleagues, especially Paul who had become quite insufferable after such a short time. Regan refused to improve her Greek pronunciation and Paul held forth endlessly about which Hollywood stars had homes here. He also loved to lecture on why the Greeks would never again rule the world, because they all they were really good for was to smoke, drink and make money off tourists. Most of them, he maintained, were surly and unfriendly and didn't speak good English. Who wouldn't be surly dealing with an arrogant loudmouth like him?

Bidding her colleagues farewell back at Athens airport, Jess boarded a small propeller-driven plane which took her just over an hour to the beautiful northern city of Ioannina. Nervously exiting the airport terminal, she spied a waiting woman she knew from photos only – her mother's sister, her aunt, her *thea*, Roula. In a heartbeat she found herself swept up in her aunt's warm embrace.

"Oh *agape mou* (My love)! You are so lovely!" exclaimed her aunt, the American accent dominating the Greek words. "Come, lets hit the road. It's only an hour and a quarter, but there's so much gorgeous scenery to see on the way."

They settled comfortably into the drive. It was as if aunt and niece had known each other all their lives. Roula of course had heard much about Jess's life, via Sally, but Jess felt there was everything still to learn about her aunt, and through this to get an understanding of her mother.

As if reading her thoughts, Roula spoke. "Such a shame your mother wouldn't come. I thought after all this time she might have come to understand and to forgive."

Jess couldn't contain herself. "Forgive what!? I just don't know anything, Thea. Mum refuses to talk to me. She's never answered my questions, all these years! Why does she hate her mother so much?"

"It's sad that she's never told you, *agape mou*. We've got enough time for me to tell you everything before you meet your *yiayia*."

And so as they drove, Thea Roula told Jess the story of a young woman, Fotoula, who was married off at the tender age of fifteen, to a local man named Giorgos. Giorgos was at least twice Fotoula's age, a man with a brutish face and little finesse about him. His idea of fun had been to force his young wife into sex whenever he wanted it, and to go wild boar hunting with his friends. Fotoula fell pregnant before she turned sixteen, and the first of two little sisters was born. Despite already loathing her husband, Fotoula fell immediately in love with her brown-eyed, olive-skinned beautiful baby and named her after the goddess of love, Afrodite. The name was often shorted to Roula in Greece. Barely recovered from a difficult birth, Fotoula again fell pregnant, this time with Soula, Jess's mother, who had happily changed her name to Sally as soon as she got away from Greece to Australia.

Sensing the story was starting to get disturbing, Roula suggested they stop off in the village of Monodendri and have a coffee. This was one of about 40 picturesque stone villages in an area known as the Zagori. How different from Santorini, thought Jess. Sure, no sparkling blue waters, but towering monolithic mountains, and breathtaking views at every turn of the road.

Over a *kafedaki glyka* (sweet Greek coffee) Roula continued the tale.

"Your *yiayia* Fotoula had it tough with my father Giorgos. She was always trying to protect your mum and me from our father's anger. He'd hit us at the drop of a hat." She paused and looked searchingly at Jess. "Are you sure you're ready for this? The next bit is not easy to hear."

Jess nodded. Nothing could be worse than not knowing.

"Three more babies were born, and all three died. Your grandmother decided to shut up shop; her poor body and heart couldn't take any more. Our father, being the beast he was, started to look at his daughters. Your mother and I were young teenagers, not much younger than Fotoula was when she was married off. Our father started paying us visits at night and threatened to slaughter us like one of his pigs if we said anything."

Unable to comprehend what she was hearing Jess began to weep. Slow silent tears ran down her cheeks. Her aunt patted her hand soothingly.

"It's ok *agape mou*. Luckily neither of us fell pregnant. Our *malaka* of a father had boasted to one of his friends what he'd done, and that man was kind, and helped both me and your mother get away from the village. After I made my way to America, I wrote to your grandmother, telling her everything, We then talked on the phone regularly, and by the way she was devastated, I knew that she had never had an inkling of what her husband had done to her beloved daughters. But your mother would never believe that her mother hadn't known. She always refused to hear that Fotoula was just as distraught by what had happened as we had been."

"That explains a lot," muttered Jess. "What happened to my grandfather?"

"Oh one day he just disappeared. Lots of rumours: killed

by one of his wild boars, fell into the gorge, murdered in an argument – who knows and who cares? Taking of the gorge, let's go while it's still light. You haven't seen anything like this."

Jess was amazed at how pragmatically her aunt retold the tale, and how she seemed to have been able to move on with her life. But she was even more amazed when, minutes later, they walked to the lookout which gave a view of a deep, majestic and awe-inspiring gorge, framed by mountains receding blue upon blue. Roula showed Jess how, when you called loudly, your voice in waves of echoes came back to you, as if from another world.

"Don't worry, we'll visit here again and go for a long walk in a day or so. First we must get to your *yiayia* before it gets dark. The village streets can be tricky at night."

They arrived at dusk in yet another quaint village, with the cute name of Mikro Papingo. The ever-watchful mountains towered over the stone cottages and the cobbled streets, as Jess and Roula abandoned the car and made their way on foot to a little house at the end of an alleyway. Grape vines framed the doorway, and a huge pot of scarlet bougainvillea stood at the entrance.

Opening the door, Roula called out, "*Eimaste spiti!*" (We're home).

A frail old lady, white hair cascading around her shoulders, sat in an oversized armchair. Her face split into a broad smile as she opened her arms to welcome the granddaughter she had never met.

৵৵৵

The five days left to Jess passed in a flurry of emotions. Anger at her mother for never having confided in her, regret that she'd not come sooner to Greece to meet her wonderful grandmother, hatred for the grandfather she'd never met, and above all love. Love for everything around her. The tiny village of 200 people was a welcoming refuge from the world and a sharp contrast to the tourist glitz of Santorini. Neighbours proudly showed Jess their gardens, brought baskets overflowing with sweet-sun-ripened tomatoes, and shared glasses of ouzo under the huge kiwi vine growing at the little village taverna. She rapidly expanded her limited Greek vocabulary, until she could almost hold down a simple conversation.

But words didn't really matter.

Except on the day she had to bid farewell to her newly-discovered family.

Fotoula was again seated in her oversized chair, and she beckoned Roula and her niece to sit by her, and asked Roula to translate.

"Your mother Soula wrote me one letter only when she arrived in Australia. She told me how much she hated me and how could I have let that happen to her. I couldn't believe what she was telling me, or that she believed I had known. How could I have let something so horrific happen to my precious girls."

She spread her hands and took in each the hand of her daughter and granddaughter, before continuing, her voice full of both emotion and resignation.

"It is such good timing that you came now. Dr Pappas says I may have only days to live. It's the cancer you know. I'll be so glad to finish with the pain." She paused, drew a deep breath and said," When Giorgos disappeared everyone thought he'd been killed or had an accident. He was killed alright. But not by one of his precious pigs. After I got Soula's letter, I invited my husband for a walk along the rim of the gorge. I told him I knew everything, and that his soul would go to hell."

She chuckled, and looked Jess in the eye. "You've walked there; you've seen the path is very narrow, very dangerous – very easy for a man to slip."

No one spoke for a long while, then the women smiled at each other, and said it was perhaps time for a small ouzo.

ଶଧଶ

Australia seemed both familiar and foreign to Jess after being in Greece. Somehow she felt like a different person. She'd poured her heart out to Sally, who seemed relieved to be able to share the burden of such weighty secrets. Thea Roula had reported that Jess's visit had somehow given her grandmother a second wind. Maybe she had more than a few days left in her.

Three days after her homecoming, Jess sat with her mother at the dinner table. Sally got up and fetched her laptop and opened the screen.

"Time for our zoom with Thea Roula and your *yiayia*," she said with happy anticipation.

**Sharon Hurst**

## Sophia

Soft curls bounce as she runs through the sun,
Over puddles and petals, her laughter's begun.
Playful and curious, she dances with glee,
Holding tight teddy, as proud as can be.
In her bright eyes, the stars seem to gleam,
A world full of wonder, a two-year-old dream.

She hums little songs only she understands,
Open arms reaching for love and for hands.
Peekaboo giggles and crumbs on her face,
Happiness follows her every place.
In her small steps, adventure takes flight,
Angels must smile as they watch her each night.

***Amanda Divers***

# Time travel

Elizabeth found an old pocket watch in a dusty antique shop while she was travelling in Paris. The owner quietly whispered with a grin, "It ticks for Love".

That evening after wandering down the small narrow streets back to her hotel, she played with this unusual looking pocket watch.

And then . . . Elizabeth woke up in 1880 in a bustling town square, where gas lamps flickered and horses clattered along the cobbled street.

Bedazzled, she looked around and was smitten by what she had only seen in old movies. Beautiful pastel fancy dresses and men in top hats.

Then a tall, elegant young man approached her.

"You look lost," he said with a deep, manly voice. She immediately looked up.

"My name is Robert Lapthorn, I am an inventor. Come with me."

As if in a trance, she followed him. He took her to his beautiful apartment, which was full of old books. It looked like a curiosity shop but was clean and very orderly.

Robert was fascinated by her modern looks, her long wavy hair, her speech, her knowledge, her intellect. Elizabeth was, for him, from a different world. They connected, laughed, danced, and kissed under the stars.

But the pocket watch was calling her. She knew she had to tell him the truth.

Robert smiled sadly. "Even borrowed time was worth every moment."

With a tearful goodbye Elizabeth turned the dial and vanished.

Back in her modern world, everything felt dull and grey. Time passed and one weekend she went to a science exhibition in London. There it was – a design by Robert Lapthorn 1880. Her heart stood still for a second.

A note beneath read "To the girl from tomorrow – I will always remember"

***Monika Nuesch***

## The die is not cast — *Ne alea iacta est*

Cast an eye on the ocean

cast a rod in the air
cast a role in the play

cast light on the subject
as the fire casts a glow
cast a vote for the free

cast metal in moulds
cast in the same mould
cast your throw calmly

cast doubt on false truth

cast a stitch off and on
cast off your qualms
cast nets far and wide

cast not pearls before swine

 never cast the first stone
nor cast away kindness
never cast callous clouts

never cast away kids
nor cast off a friend
never cast a long shadow

the die is not cast
as you cast off your boat
never cast it adrift

cast around for a plan
cast around in your search
cast aside cruelty

never cast aspersions
nor cast schemes in concrete
cast out the uncouth

cast your statement in reason
cast your longing with love
cast a spell over me.

**Ann Simic**

## The Forest Ghoulie

What makes a monster scary? Is it just because he's hairy? Or his colour? Or his size? Or his dark and watchful eyes? Whatever can it be? Let's follow on ... and see.

When Danny was a little boy and going off to school, he would travel through the dark and scary Forest of the... Ghoulie

Ghoulie lives deep underground in a dark and musty cave, and if he's looking out at you, you'll have to be quite brave!

Did Ghoulie grab your shoulder? Did you feel him pull your clothes? Or was it just a blackberry that scratched your arm and nose?

When rain creates a puddle, you can see into his lair. He has whiskers in his ears. He has short and spiky hair.

The forest, dark and mossy, Smells of mushrooms, and of trees, and of Ghoulie's earthy body wafting gently on the breeze.

In the mud: Are they his footprints- those grooves, both long and deep? I wonder how their shape is made from the soles of Ghoulie's feet.

The bones of Ghoulie's dinners in the branches, high, are hung up where the birds are nesting, to be bleached out by the Sun.

When Forest Ghoulie stands up tall, the possums quake with fright. But, luckily, this happens in the middle of the night.

And, when heavy storms are raging, you can hear his mournful cry as thunderclaps roll all around and lightning splits the sky.

Is that the wind that's blowing with such a gale's force?

Or are the branches bending flat because of Ghoulie's snores?
Don't wake the Forest Ghoulie by kicking at his toes! He doesn't act too kindly when he's woken from a doze.
Tiptoe through Ghoulie's forest. The sound of running feet awakens him with promises of something fresh... to eat!
Then, as Danny became older, He could see (to his elation) there was really nothing scary but his own imagination!
Raaah!

**Su Lam**

# A Christmas tale

'Tis Xmas day and the Richmond rellies are here to stay, There was Oll, her husband Bob and her two sisters, Maggie and Bertha with their husbands Gordon and Keith. Outside the temperature was rising while inside the wood stove blazed.

Oll served the meal. Although money was tight, she managed to serve roast goose, potatoes, pumpkin, parsnips, peas, all fresh from the garden. When it came time to serve the plum pudding, the children were agog, for they knew there would be shiny sixpences hidden in the ingredients.

Dinner over, the men, beer in hand, listened to the cricket, while Oll, Maggie and Bertha washed the dishes in the old tin dish.

It was just after lunch when Bob said to Gordon and Keith, 'Come outside, I've got something to show you.'

Bob led the men to the rickety old shed down the backyard. He pushed open the door and there, in all its glory, stood a motorbike and side car.

'Gor, it's a Red Indian,' Gordon said. 'However did you come by it?'

'It arrived by train,' Bob said with a smirk on his face.

'What do you mean it arrived by train?'

'It was in the guard's van addressed to me.'

'Have you ridden it?" Keith asked.

'Not yet . . . I'm not quite sure how to ride it.'

Bob wheeled the Red Indian out of the shed, its duco gleaming. He pushed it through the back gate and out onto the gravel road.

'Anyone for a ride?' Bob asked.

Gordon, hesitant, cocked his leg over the pillion seat and wiggled his bum to make himself more comfortable., while Keith hopped into the side car. 'Plop', the dog landed on Keith's lap.

'You keep your eyes on the road,' Oll admonished.

Bob pulled out the throttle but the bike refused to budge.

'Do you want a push?' Johnnie asked, a cheeky grin on his face.

Bob, irritated by the smart-arsed Johnnie, pulled out the throttle and the bike burst into life and took off in a crooked line down the road.

'Hope they arrive home in one piece,' Bertha said as the sisters walked inside. Later that day, there was no sign of the men.

'I wonder where they've got to,' Oll said.

But as the day ended and dusk began to fall, the men were to be heard coming through the back gate. The first to arrive was Bob (nothing wrong with him except for a few scratches – he could hold his grog); next came Gordon, his face the colour of puce (he never could hold his drink); and last of all, Keith, who leant against the door to support himself.

'Where in the hell have you been?' Maggie demanded. 'We thought you'd been in an accident.'

She gazed at the men. 'And which of you drove the bike home?'

Bob hiccupped. 'No one. We pushed it all the way home from the distillery.'

Bertha and Maggie burst into laughter, but Oll didn't as much as smile. All she could think of was her drunken father and the dread of him coming home after a drinking bout.

**Lorraine Doney**

## A fragile friendship

We talk-
About the weather
and our daily events
Skimming surfaces.
Sometimes
  I feel
    I could
      fall
Between the depths
Of the vague spaces
Of the pauses
Of all that
You will not say
and what I cannot ask.
Both hesitant
To unfold layers
Of a fragile friendship.

***Aileen Heal***

# The most troubling challenge for modern humanity:
## Disconnection in an age of hyperconnectivity

In an era where technology has made communication instantaneous and global, one might assume that humanity has never been more connected. Social media, video calls, and instant messaging bridge distances that once seemed insurmountable. Yet paradoxically, modern humanity faces a crisis of profound disconnection – not from each other technologically, but emotionally, socially, and spiritually. This disconnection manifests in rising mental health issues, political polarization, environmental detachment, and a weakening sense of community. Despite living in an age of information and opportunity, people increasingly report feelings of loneliness, anxiety, and purposelessness. This emotional dislocation is arguably the most troubling challenge of our time.

### The illusion of connection

Social media platforms promise to keep people connected, but often only foster superficial interactions. A curated online persona can replace authentic self-expression, while "likes" and "followers" stand in for genuine relationships. Real-life social bonds – family dinners, neighbourhood gatherings, spontaneous conversations – are being replaced with screen time. Ironically, the more we immerse ourselves in digital networks, the more we can feel isolated from meaningful human contact. Loneliness has become a public health crisis, with its health risks comparable to smoking or obesity.

## The erosion of shared reality

Another layer of disconnection comes from the breakdown of a shared understanding of truth. The internet has democratized information, but also created echo chambers and disinformation bubbles. People now live in separate realities, guided by algorithms designed to maximize engagement, not truth. This has led to dangerous levels of political polarization, mistrust in institutions, and civil unrest. When people cannot agree on basic facts, constructive dialogue and collective progress become nearly impossible.

## Alienation from nature

Modern lifestyles have also deepened humanity's disconnection from the natural world. Urbanization, consumer culture, and environmental exploitation have created a barrier between people and the ecosystems they depend on. Many children grow up without ever planting a seed or seeing a starry sky free of light pollution. This alienation undermines the motivation to address climate change or protect biodiversity, further threatening our planet's health and our own survival.

## Loss of meaning and community

Traditional sources of meaning – religion, family, civic duty, and shared cultural narratives—have been eroded or fractured in many societies. While secularism and individualism offer freedom, they can also leave people adrift without a framework for understanding their place in the world. In the absence of community and shared purpose, people may turn to extremism, consumerism, or nihilism. Mental health challenges such as depression, anxiety, and suicide are rising across the globe, especially among younger generations.

## A way forward

Despite these daunting challenges, there is hope. Recognizing the crisis of disconnection is the first step toward healing it. Solutions must begin with rebuilding authentic relationships – through education that fosters emotional intelligence, community-based initiatives that encourage cooperation, and urban planning that prioritizes human interaction over convenience. Technology must be harnessed not just to connect devices, but to truly connect people. Meanwhile, environmental education and stewardship can restore our bond with the natural world, reminding us that we are not apart from nature, but a part of it.

Most importantly, humanity must rediscover shared values – empathy, truth, compassion, and responsibility – that transcend political, cultural, and economic divides. Only through conscious reconnection – with each other, with nature, and with ourselves – can we overcome the quiet crisis that underlies so many of today's global problems.

*Peter Levy*

## morning on the bay

feathered limbs spread
wider than a tall man is high
soaring searching
wheeling and diving
with white plumage
made brighter
by black-barred wings
soft yellow face
piercing eyes
perfect heads
for spearing the water

. . . but from a distance
a ballet
of pirouettes and circling
crowding cloud of motion
crying choir of commotion

. . . but from a distance
a quiet dance
of death to the chosen fish
grudgingly acknowledged
by the men in small boats
with a similar wish

**Paul Downton**

## I'm in love

I'm in love with the idea of loving
Not in the look at me look at me sort of
way There seems to be so much of that
these days I prefer the loving, caring sort
of way
more enduring sort of way as this makes sense to me

Just as I am, acknowledging all parts of myself and there
are a few parts as everyone has them
Maybe that's why it's a challenge to love some people
I think If I was on stage
there would be many of me on the stage
All a bit different, all unique, all wearing different
costumes to describe the personality
Then I think of Shakespeare and how he was so right
How to bring that higher love to the stage of your life
To the earth and its people that need much love with
boundaries to protect thee
I'm in love with the idea of being in love and the idea of
them loving me
Not just in a romantic sense though that is nice too, but
a deeper sort that lasts the good and the bad
Growing, challenging and loving
More daring and more enduring
The sun doesn't come out every day Not always blue
skies and rainbows I'm in love with ideals and standards
I'm in love with what the great masters of right thinking
have to say
I'm in love with the sunshine, with swimming, yoga,
movement and my hands in clay

I'm in love when I swing the golf club and it feels so right and it lands in the right spot
I'm in love with writing words, sometimes I wonder where such lines of words come from and all for the right reasons
I'm in love with a purpose for positive change for me and thee
Oh how the great masters were so right
And of course, the most important is to love thyself and thee
In a grander way

**Rose Lumbaca Crane**

# My nightmare as an Au Pair

To be an Au Pair is a very old tradition – for as long as I can remember. As a teenager I always had a great desire to learn languages. My wish was to travel the world. At high school I learned French and Italian as it was part of the school curriculum. I just knew I wanted more than a little knowledge. I wanted to be more fluent and have great conversations with the people I met from foreign countries. So, when I finished my college year, I instinctively knew that my next step was to become an Au Pair in the French speaking area of Switzerland.

I mentioned it one afternoon after school to my mother. She was in a way dismayed and surprised at such an idea. Immediately her response was "You will have to look after screaming children" which she knew I had no desire to do. She also said, "Why lower yourself to such a low status," when you are already almost fluent in French?" She also mentioned long hours for little pay. But nothing would deter me from my adventure to experience that traditional custom.

I said very convincingly to my mother, "Surely you don't have to just look after children. I believe there might be some other opportunities available. I will investigate what is on offer."

I telephoned the Au Pair agency. No children to look after was my first priority. My ideal place would be in Lausanne or Geneva - no little township. The lady in charge took note of my desires. She said as soon as something suitable comes up she will contact me. Everything sounded so reassuring and right.

About six weeks later I had received a telephone message from the agency. I was beaming with excitement. I had the biggest smile ever. Everything sounded so perfect - just what I had envisioned. No toddlers to look after - just a couple. The position was with an elderly aristocratic French couple – a husband and wife – located in the French-speaking city of Lausanne, they also had a holiday house with a swimming pool near Avignon in France, I had been told. I then envisioned myself going for lots of swims in my spare time. My duties were to look after the house, clean and help the madam to prepare the food. This sounded to my ear just fabulous. I said to the manager that I would discuss it with my parents and that I would call her back. Well, I had all my questions answered and I was satisfied with the outcome.

After lengthy discussion with my parents, they allowed me to go by train to Lausanne for an interview. It was a very long trip – I travelled from one side of the country to the other. The train took four hours each way. The scenic train ride was a delight to my eyes and senses. It was my first visit to this beautiful city which I'd only known from photos, postcards and books in the library.

When the train arrived in Lausanne, I immediately saw Mrs. Trussaud, she stood out from the crowd on the platform. She held up a board with my full name. Her clothing looked tailored and expensive and her strict hairstyle coiffed as if she had just stepped out from the most expensive hairdresser in town - every single hair was in its place. She came across as very formal and haughty to me. We exchanged some small talk and then we walked swiftly to her car. To my surprise it was a bright red Porsche 911. What an exquisite car model. I'd never seen one before - just in magazines. My brother worked for a German car company, so there were many car magazines in our household. Can you imagine how impressive that first encounter with Madame Trussaud was? It was my first (and last) ride in a Porsche. An experience I will never forget. We had some pleasant conversation in French. I loved the sound of the French language The weather was just splendid as it was near the end of May, and everything was in full bloom. The city was bustling with cars and trams. Everywhere was so colourful to me and so exotic.

After a while driving, we arrived at their grand mansion. It was like a Hollywood Villa with a beautiful ornate gate and an expansive driveway. I could see the gardener busy keeping flowers trimmed. It felt as if I had just walked onto a movie set. Everything seemed like a dream to me. The butler opened the door, just like in the TV series from Downton Abbey, but of course on a much smaller scale. I stepped into another world. The interior design was so overwhelming, large antique furniture, gold gilded paintings, with large fresh flower arrangements. Ornaments so exquisite I would be too scared to touch them. They had definitely travelled around the world in luxury. The husband greeted me in the lounge. He was tall and slim and like his wife, exuded an aura of wealth that I had never seen before.

**Interview with Mr and Mrs Trussaud**
The interview was very formal and business like. We were served afternoon tea with perfectly cut sandwiches and some delicacies from a fancy French patisserie. I

did enjoy the whole experience tremendously. Being an impressionable young girl just over 18 years young. My eyes kept wandering to make sure I didn't miss any interesting objects d'art. It was eye candy wherever I looked.

After what felt like a lengthy interrogation about my family background and my own background, the interview came to an end. Madame Trussaud leaned forward and locked me straight into my eyes.

"We would like you to be our personal assistant for the 3 months we are staying at our holiday house."

I already knew in my mind that it was exactly what I wanted to do. I said that I was interested in the position, and that I would discuss it with my parents and let them know within 2 days. I think the Madame could see that I was enthusiastic to take on this Au Pair position. What I liked the most – no children involved, only to look after the husband and wife. Which meant general housework and helping her prepare delicious French food. She also said she would have regular guests for lunch including the Pastor from the village. How lovely would that be – meeting interesting new people to talk to and learn the art of fine French cooking. I have always liked cooking and trying new food and to this day I still find great enjoyment in this creative endeavour.

We said our formal goodbyes and then the butler drove me to the station in a very big and beautiful classic car. I quickly gave my mother a call before I got on the train, I said all went well and that I would arrive just after dinner. We can talk about it when I get home. I must go as the train will arrive shortly. What a wonderful feeling that I'd been accepted for this job. Deep down I wondered how many other girls had applied for this.

The train arrived punctually – as every train always does in

Switzerland. The train ride was just magnificent, passing by the glistening Lake Geneva. Surrounded by vineyards and cute wooden houses nestled around the lake. I could see France on the other side of the lake. The sunshine and the blue skies were glorious. I took a book with me to read, but I was too mesmerised by the beauty of my home country, that this moment wasn't the right time for reading. I was in a dreaming mode; I would commence employment in 2 weeks. Arrive first in Lausanne, then travel to Avignon by car to their holiday house with its own swimming pool! This was going to be so much fun! Sunshine and warm weather every day. I just adore warm or even hot weather. As a joke I would always say to my Australian friends I am made for hot weather. We always have a laugh about that.

The comfortable train ride home went quickly. I guess all this contemplation and admiring the landscape. I hadn't previously been that much outside my area and now I was travelling through the other side of my country. There was certainly so much to see. I knew on that journey that one day I will have to do a tour of the whole of Switzerland by train.

When I saw my mother at the train platform I couldn't wait to get out and tell her all about it. It was the first time I had travelled alone on such a long trip. We hugged each other affectionately, I loved her so much - she was so perfect in every way. I could speak to her about anything that was concerning to me. I was so blessed that I had in my mind, that I have the best Mama in the world.

After a few minutes we arrived home. My dinner was warm and ready to eat. But for me it was more important to tell my story. Both my parents were listening very carefully and once I got it all out, that's when they asked me some serious questions. Mother still couldn't understand why I wanted to be a servant/cleaner for an elderly rich couple. My response was to learn the language even better, experience a different family dynamic, a different culture, a new lifestyle and to learn a new way of cooking. And it's a young person's adventure to travel and see new places. They were all positive arguments why I wanted to do this. I have always been a bit strong willed in relation to what I wanted to do and generally, I went ahead with it. Another good selling point I had was that it was arranged through an agency and everybody is screened.

Finally, I got my parents' agreement, and my Mama told me that she had spoken to the agency to make sure that everything would be safe for her daughter. So now I could ring Madame Trussaud to say that I will go with them to France. We discussed the finer details in relation to what I should bring, when we leave for their holiday vacation home. The agency organised all the paperwork so that everybody had a copy.

## Farewell to my parents

I started packing with the guidance of my mother. A medium size suitcase and a little blue rucksack - which by miracle I still have to this day. That's where I put my essentials like notebooks, pencils, reading material, some lollies and of course a sturdy water bottle and some deliciously prepared sandwiches from my Mama. The big day had arrived for me - all the details had been carefully planned. I made one last phone call to Madame Trussaud to tell her my arrival time in Lausanne. Mother took me to the railway station. I really hate farewells; they always trigger so many emotions in me. That would be my first time away from my parents for many months. I started shedding some tears and then I could see my mother started as well. We hugged and kissed and said our goodbyes. Mother reminded me not to forget to call as soon as I arrived. I opened the train window and waved wildly, blew kisses and assured her that I would write and call regularly.

Now I was on my own with my luggage carefully arranged around me. I looked out the window and saw my town passing by very quickly. Everything looked so luscious and green. The weather was simply divine. Blue sky and warm temperature. It was the month of June and the start of the European summer. For a moment I closed my eyes - I felt happy and full of joy and high expectation for the experience awaiting me. My thoughts were how lucky I was to be the chosen one.

## Arrival in Lausanne

After a wonderful but long journey I arrived early that afternoon. The butler, Monsieur Salvignon, was waiting for me on the platform. I felt a bit like royalty in that split second. He greeted me and helped me with my luggage. All I had to carry was the brand-new handbag my mum had purchased for me as a present. I loved that bag, it had so many different compartments and secret little hiding places. Just exactly what I wanted. I was so grateful I could choose my own handbag – it was quite a bit more expensive than my mother had wanted to spend. I said it was my birthday and Christmas present, and she agreed.

The butler and I walked in a fast pace to the designated carpark. It was that big beautiful lavish car again; this time I took more notice of which brand of car it was. It was a Bentley in a dark maroon colour with beige leather seating. Total opulence and so spacious. I sat at the back with just my handbag. The luggage was stored in the boot; so large that a human body could lay down in comfort.

After a short drive we arrived at their lovely estate. Madame and Monsieur Trussaud were waiting for me; they greeted me briefly and then the butler showed me to my room where I could have a rest until I was called for dinner. I looked around the room, it was tastefully decorated as a guestroom. It had all the little treats you can ask for – I even had my own bathroom, how cool is that I thought. I looked outside the window and saw a perfectly manicured garden and oh! a swimming pool was there as well. I went to the other window and there was a tennis court. This family was obviously very wealthy.

I decided to have a rest for a little while then have a shower before going down to dinner. I was just having a shower when I heard a loud knock on my door.

"Mademoiselle Monique, dinner in one hour."

"*Oui merci*," I responded.

Great, that gives me enough time to explore and admire the gorgeous garden. It was a fairytale garden with precisely manicured flowers and bushes all around. I had never been in a garden like this.

Time for dinner - I could hear the bell. I approached the entrance and was waiting for someone to show me the way to the dining room. Deep down I wanted to see and discover every single room, but of course I would not be allowed - I was not in a museum. So dutifully I waited till Madame called me by name. Everything was so courtly and rigid. The dining table was attractively presented with pressed white linen serviettes, silverware and fresh flowers from the garden.

There was not a lot of conversation. In my family we always had lively, fun conversation at dinner. Here it was so quiet and strange to me. I somehow felt like an outsider.

I did not dare to speak except to say *"bon appetit."* To my amazement husband and wife addressed each other only using formal language – which in French is *vous* and not the common form of *tu*. That was most unusual. I never dared to ask about it and to this day I still remember this unusual etiquette.

We finished the delicious three course meal which was light and with lots of interesting flavour. It was like a menu from a French restaurant.

Madame said, "Tomorrow we get up at 8 am. Breakfast is at 9 am and departure for the holiday house at 10 am."

I got the courage to ask how long it would take to get there. She said it was about 500 km, and we would arrive in late afternoon. I said, *"merci beaucoup"* and *"bonne nuit"* and then went to my bedroom. It was a long day, and I fell asleep very quickly.

I was woken up by my old-fashioned orange alarm clock, which made a lot of noise. We all sat down for breakfast at 9 am. The breakfast consisted of croissants, butter, jam, a variety of seasonal fruit, yoghurt, some nice strong coffee and a glass of orange juice. Just like the night before not many words were spoken.

By exactly 10am the Bentley was fully packed with everyone's luggage. The long drive to Avignon began on yet another sunny day with the butler waving us goodbye. I sat at the back with lots of space and I had all my luggage next to me. The windows were wide and large so I could enjoy the scenery to the maximum. I found it very strange that they did not include me in their conversation. I was so eager to tell them about my special holidays I had with my parents. It felt like I wasn't even there with them in the car. They totally ignored me. I wanted to chat so much, but maybe the right moment just hadn't come yet. So, I thought I'd better be patient.

Finally, they addressed me after a few hours of driving. "We will stop very soon for lunch."

It was a pretty little French village with old stone buildings, it was so enchanting to me, I loved this different architecture. Madame ordered sandwiches and a bottle of Perrier mineral water for everyone. I commented how pretty it looks and that I am delighted to be here. I received no comments or response at all. It made me a bit upset and sad at how they could ignore a friendly joyful comment from a young girl. But I thought, I have got to be strong in my head and not let that interfere with my thinking. When we arrived in Avignon we stopped for a big supermarket; we needed to buy some food. Where their holiday house is, there was only one small convenience store. After the supermarket we drove through the old historic city – it was like an old medieval town, with lots of people, I guess a very popular tourist destination. From there we drove up a hill past the big bridge of Avignon. There is even a song about that famous bridge. It's called: *Sur Le Pont D'Avignon*.

## Arrival at a villa near Avignon

I started to see less and less houses. It seemed like an eternity – very small dirt roads going through all those tiny villages.

At last we arrived. They parked outside their stone walled villa. The colours were all in white and cream. The entrance had a heavy wooden door like a traditional church door. It was an amazing place; everything was so white and fresh. When the big heavy wooden doors opened, I could see a gorgeous outdoor area. A nice size swimming pool on my left and a pretty pergola surrounded with luscious large grapevines. Everything looked so perfect like a tourist brochure from the Mediterranean Sea.

We unpacked the shopping and then I asked politely if I could call my parents to let them know that we had arrived safely. To my total shock Madame told me I would have to wait until the morning when her husband goes to the post office to collect their mail. Again, I said patiently that my parents expected a call from me tonight. Madame answered very coldly to me that I would have to wait till tomorrow. I said immediately I will pay for the call. She turned around very abruptly with an unfriendly lock on her face and just walked away. Her husband didn't say a word; all he murmured was "I'll show you to your room" He carried my small suitcase; up the winding small staircase leading up to my very meagre room.

It was more than basic. A single bed, a small table with a chair, an old, damaged wardrobe and an odd-looking bedside table. It looked poor in comparison to the rest of the house which was exquisitely decorated in the finest antiques and ornaments. I felt like I was in a bad movie set, not like I had envisaged. My first thought was I am not sure if I am going to like it here. But very quickly I put that thought away - it was not a nice feeling. I unpacked my few belongings then I laid on the old bed. The mattress was old shapeless and uncomfortable, but I needed a rest.

It didn't take long before Madame Trussaud called me "Monique, Monique". She said she didn't like the German version of my name, and that Monique sounded much nicer. It didn't bother me too much as it sounded melodic, and I liked the French language.

Madame Trussaud said, "We're going to have some supper, can you come down."

She told me what I needed to do, and I obliged. We were sitting outside under that large pergola surrounded by scented flowers and those bright green grapevines and next to that inviting swimming pool. The sights for me were a true delight – so different from my familiar homeland. At the table again, not many words were exchanged. I kept to myself. I was bringing the food and afterwards she explained how she wanted the dishes and kitchen to be cleaned. I just agreed.

They said, "*Bonne nuit*". She then reminded me that her husband would be leaving at 10am to go to the post office. I just said , "Oui, I will be ready to go with him".

I finished all the dishes and the cleaning up and then I was glad to go into my own small room. My shower was downstairs at the very end of the hallway which meant lots of walking especially at night. But I had to put up with it - there was no other choice. I couldn't wait till I could jump into bed. It was quite a long exhausting day, and I was not sure of what to think of it. I was lying restless in bed thinking of my parents, as they would be waiting for my phone call, and I couldn't ring them. I hoped they would understand - I would have to come up with a good plausible story. While I was thinking of a story, I finally fell into a deep sleep.

After breakfast I left with Monsieur Trussaud to go to the post office in a larger village. He told me he goes there weekly to collect his mail. I couldn't wait to call my parents to tell them that we arrived safely. The phone rang, and my mother answered very quickly. Before she could say anything, I said in a very convincing tone that there is no phone in the house, because it's an old stone building and they are there only occasionally. So, I told her that I could only call her on a weekly basis when we went to the post office. She seemed alright with that – probably because I sounded very bubbly and happy. Deep down though, I was not alright with that deception. But I knew my mama would never know the truth – it will always remain my secret.

## My dream is shattered

We returned to the holiday house. The weather was sunny and warm. I so wanted to take a dip in the pool - maybe later after I have done some housework. Madame called me in a demanding tone. She told me today we start to clean the whole house. There was, of course, a lot of dust accumulated since they were last there. She explained to me in detail what I had to start with. She showed me all the cleaning products and gave me strict instructions as to how she wanted everything cleaned.

The task was enormous and overwhelming. The house had so many rooms. There were four large bedrooms and my upstairs Rapunzel room. There was also a large kitchen, a butler's pantry, a large dining room and an even bigger living area. I had never seen such a large house in all my young years. Every room was entirely decorated with antique furniture, elaborate ornaments and lots of paintings. This was going to be a tremendous workload. The whole situation of cleaning the house was truly overwhelming for me. I asked naively if there was someone else coming to help me.

"Of course, not," Madame said in a harsh tone. "That's what you are here for."

I did not respond – I was in total disbelief. She ushered me around to tell me what job to do first and then, after a while, came to check up if I was doing it to her satisfaction.

It was so humiliating. After many hours of hard labour, I wanted a break, so I sat down on one of the exquisite sofas. The material felt so luxurious when I gently touched it with my hand.

As I sat there daydreaming, suddenly I heard Madame yell at me, "Get up and keep cleaning."

In that moment I was so traumatised how badly I was treated on my first day. I was just a young girl and such treatment as someone yelling at me was something I was not used to. This was my first time away from home for a lengthy period – and in a foreign country with strangers. She spoke harshly to me: "You are here to work, not on a holiday."

Being so young and inexperienced I didn't know what to say. She made me labour very hard for long hours daily. I had no energy left to even read a book when I was back in my simple sparse bedroom. What made me sad, was I had no one to talk to.

"How can I improve my French if I can't talk to anyone?" I asked myself. My happiness turned into sorrow. I felt as though I had become like a robot – all I could say was "Oui Madame" and nothing else.

After about two weeks, Madame announced that her three adult children would be coming with their spouses to stay for a while. My thoughts turned to, oh no more work for myself. I was already exhausted with the hard labour she was ordering me to do. My day would start at 7.30 am. Now with eight people living here and I alone had to do all the cleaning. I was just their servant – or a better description, their slave. Nobody would engage in a conversation with me, I felt invisible to them. All they did was order me around. I so missed talking to people. I had to eat by myself in a hidden corner away from the family gathering. Nobody was interested in me or even asked how I was feeling. I became very sad, and my cheerful personality lost some of its spark. After dinner there were so many dishes to do, I remember I never finished before 10 pm. It was all done by hand – no dishwasher – just me silenced in the big kitchen. The family gathered outside under that gorgeous pergola, having drinks and laughing, and using the pool - which I was never allowed to do. I was nearly in tears, thinking of my mother and how right she had been. It had truly become a nightmare for me. I could never leave the house - as a matter of fact I was locked up in that villa. I knew I had to escape somehow.

**Planning my escape**
In my weekly calls to Mama, I made sure that I sounded cheerful. I did not want her to worry. I achieved that well, what a good actress I thought I was. Later in life I did that as an amateur on stage. I totally fell in love with acting. My imagination was going wild concocting how I could escape my nightmare. Lots of thinking and preparing. I checked the whole house for an escape route, as they always locked the house when away. The cellar had a lot of stuff that I rummaged through, I found an open window behind some boxes with no steel across the window. It looked large enough – I measured it with my body. I wanted to make sure that I could take my three travel pieces back with me.

My heart was bouncing full of hope. I could see that it would work. Now the only obstacle was, that I could only leave when nobody was around. My next step was to find out about buses. The Monday during our weekly post office visit I would talk to the staff and find out about the bus timetable. In this tiny village I discovered that there was only one bus a week, on Friday at 10 am and it went directly to Avignon. It all sounded promising in my mind. I could have everything ready and packed – I would write them a letter explaining why I left. That would be a shock to them, I thought.

With all that information under my belt I had a good plan for my escape. So then, I prayed - that they would be away on a daytrip. I overheard a conversation whilst I was serving dinner, that they were going to a large antique fair outside Avignon and they were planning to be there on the first day of opening - a Friday! The whole family was obsessed with antiques. My heart was pounding so hard when I heard this exciting news.

Madame told me that this Friday just serve them coffee and croissant for breakfast at 8 am. I just said "Oui bien sûr" I was so excited and nervous at the same time, that night I couldn't sleep. I got up at 6 am and organised their breakfast and when they left, I wished them a wonderful day. I ran up to my room and wrote them a letter stating how I truly felt and how they had treated me like a slave. I was very strong with my words. I left the letter on the wobbly wooden table in my room.

My three luggage pieces were already packed the night before, I didn't want to waste any time putting my belongings together. The house was clear now. My body was shaking when I went to the cellar door with all my bags. I first shoved my small suitcase out of the window then my rucksack and then I put my handbag across my chest. It was a hard fall, but I was very athletic. All went well. I grabbed my belongings and then walked swiftly away from this horrible place. One more time I looked back at the white stone villa and then I continued my daring escape, I felt secure and safe, knowing they were far away on their treasure hunts for antiques.

The landscape was very dry and sparse. I passed a few houses, there was nobody around. It felt like a ghost town. The sun was pleasant and the sky a true ultra marine colour with no clouds. It was an easy 10-minute walk to the tiny village. I felt calm as I arrived far too early at the bus stop. As my father would say "better early than too late". I have always lived by that philosophy.

From a distance I saw the bus coming. I had so many feelings in my stomach. As I paid for my ticket, I could feel my hands trembling. The conductor could sense my uneasiness, but I was relieved he didn't ask any questions. I sat far away from the driver. I was the only passenger. I closed my eyes with a content smile and thought "Free at last . . . "

*Monika Nuesch*

## Sacred unravelling

The truth is —
In order to rebuild,
you must fall apart first.
To surrender to the sacred unravelling
in the process of shedding the old self.
To fully allow the ache of becoming.
Feel the tug towards more authenticity.
Quietly knowing . . .
You cannot go back to who you once were.

***Aileen Heal***

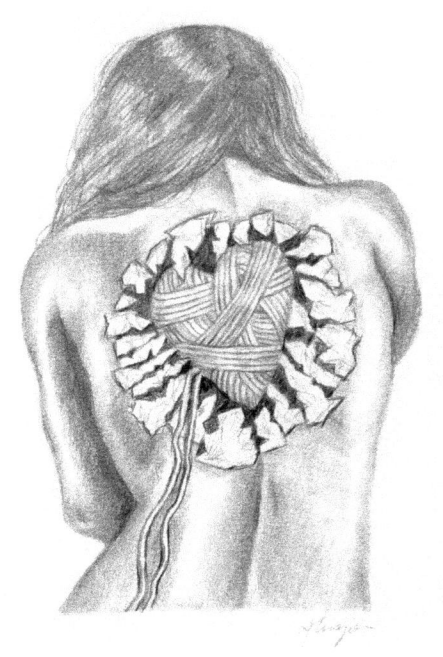

www.ingramcontent.com/pod-product-compliance
Lightning Source LLC
Chambersburg PA
CBHW040638100526
44583CB00037B/3056